DYLAN FOX

API Development Fundamentals With Flask

Copyright © 2024 by Dylan Fox

All rights reserved. No part of this publication may be reproduced, stored or transmitted in any form or by any means, electronic, mechanical, photocopying, recording, scanning, or otherwise without written permission from the publisher. It is illegal to copy this book, post it to a website, or distribute it by any other means without permission.

First edition

This book was professionally typeset on Reedsy.
Find out more at reedsy.com

Contents

Chapter 1: Introduction to API Development — 1
Chapter 2: Setting Up Flask for API Development — 10
Chapter 3: Understanding Flask Routing and Views — 21
Chapter 4: Flask Request and Response Cycle — 30
Chapter 5: Database Integration with Flask — 40
Chapter 6: Handling Errors and Exceptions in Flask APIs — 50
Chapter 7: Authentication and Authorization in Flask APIs — 57
Chapter 8: Building a RESTful API with Flask — 67
Chapter 9: Testing and Debugging Flask APIs — 75
Chapter 10: Flask Extensions for API Development — 84
Chapter 11: Deploying Flask APIs — 94
Chapter 12: API Rate Limiting and Caching in Flask — 105
Chapter 13: Handling File Uploads and Downloads — 112
Chapter 14: Advanced Flask API Features — 119
Chapter 15: Version Control and CI/CD for Flask APIs — 128
Chapter 16: Monitoring and Logging Flask APIs — 136
Chapter 17: Scaling Flask APIs — 142
Chapter 18: Conclusion and Next Steps — 149

Chapter 1: Introduction to API Development

API development has become a foundational skill in modern software engineering, especially as systems become more complex and interconnected. This chapter introduces the fundamental concepts of Application Programming Interfaces (APIs) and explains how they serve as a bridge between different applications, services, and platforms. We will explore types of APIs, understand core concepts such as endpoints, HTTP methods, and status codes, and provide an overview of Flask, a powerful yet lightweight framework used to develop APIs in Python.

1.1 What is an API?

An Application Programming Interface (API) is a set of rules and protocols that allow one application to communicate with another. APIs are the connectors that enable software to interact with other software, providing a standard method for requests and responses. They define the kinds of calls or requests that can be made, how to make them, the data formats to use, and the conventions to follow.

APIs are crucial in modern software development, as they allow different systems to share data and functionality without needing to know the inner workings of each other. Instead of directly accessing a database, for example, an application can interact with an API to retrieve the necessary data, making it easier to maintain, scale, and secure applications.

Real-World Example of API Usage

Consider a mobile weather app. It doesn't gather weather data directly; instead, it fetches that data from a weather service API. This API interacts with the weather service's database, retrieves the relevant data, and provides it in a format that the mobile app can display to the user. The app, in turn, makes a request to the API whenever the user needs updated weather information, and the API returns the appropriate response.

Key Functions of an API

- **Abstraction**: APIs simplify interactions by abstracting the underlying system complexities. Developers do not need to understand the internal details of the systems they are interacting with.
- **Interoperability**: APIs enable software developed on different platforms and in different languages to communicate seamlessly.
- **Modularity**: APIs encourage modular development. Instead of building everything from scratch, developers can leverage existing APIs to add features quickly.
- **Scalability**: APIs facilitate scalability by allowing components to interact with each other in a controlled manner.

1.2 Types of APIs: REST vs. SOAP

Two of the most common architectures for web APIs are **REST (Representational State Transfer)** and **SOAP (Simple Object Access Protocol)**. While both architectures serve similar purposes, they differ in the way they structure, transmit, and process data.

REST (Representational State Transfer)

REST is an architectural style that defines a set of constraints for creating web services. It emphasizes a stateless, client-server model where every resource is identified by a unique URL. REST APIs typically use standard HTTP methods, such as GET, POST, PUT, DELETE, and PATCH, to perform operations on resources. REST is known for being lightweight and easy to use.

Key Characteristics of REST APIs

- **Stateless**: Each API request is independent, and the server does not store any context or state between requests. This simplifies server design and improves scalability.
- **Resource-Oriented**: Resources, such as users, orders, or products, are identified by URLs, and operations on those resources are performed using HTTP methods.
- **JSON/XML Data Format**: REST APIs often return data in a human-readable format like JSON or XML, with JSON being the most common due to its simplicity and compatibility with many programming languages.
- **Caching**: REST supports caching to improve the performance of API responses.

Advantages of REST

- Lightweight and fast.
- Easy to understand and implement.
- Flexible with various data formats (though JSON is most common).
- Suitable for mobile and web applications due to its low bandwidth usage.

Example:
A typical REST API call might look like this:
GET /users/123
This request asks for the details of the user with the ID of 123. The server responds with a JSON object containing the user's information.
SOAP (Simple Object Access Protocol)
SOAP is a protocol that defines a set of rules for structuring messages. It relies on XML to format data and typically uses HTTP, SMTP, or other protocols for message transmission. SOAP is more rigid and complex compared to REST but provides additional features, such as built-in error handling and security standards.

Key Characteristics of SOAP APIs

- **XML-Based**: SOAP uses XML for message formatting, making it verbose but highly structured.
- **Built-In Security**: SOAP supports WS-Security, making it ideal for applications requiring strict security standards, such as financial systems.
- **Standardized**: SOAP follows strict standards, ensuring consistency across different platforms.
- **Supports Both Synchronous and Asynchronous Calls**: SOAP allows for more flexibility in communication patterns compared to REST.

Advantages of SOAP

- Robust security and built-in error handling.
- Standardized, making it easier to ensure compatibility.
- Ideal for enterprise-level applications that need high reliability and security.

Example:
A SOAP request might look like this:

```xml
Copy code
<soapenv:Envelope
xmlns:soapenv="http://schemas.xmlsoap.org/soap/envelope/"
xmlns:web="http://www.example.com/webservice">
    <soapenv:Header/>
    <soapenv:Body>
       <web:GetUser>
          <web:userId>123</web:userId>
       </web:GetUser>
    </soapenv:Body>
</soapenv:Envelope>
```

This XML-based request asks for the user with an ID of 123, and the server responds with an XML structure containing the user information.

REST vs. SOAP: A Comparison

Feature	REST	SOAP
Data Format	JSON (mostly), XML, etc.	XML only
Protocol	HTTP, HTTPS	HTTP, SMTP, others
Complexity	Simple and lightweight	More complex and rigid
Caching	Supported	Not supported
Security	Must be implemented	Built-in (WS-Security)
Bandwidth	Lower	Higher due to XML overhead
Use Case	Web, mobile applications	Enterprise applications requiring high security and transaction reliability

1.3 Understanding API Endpoints and Routes

API endpoints and routes form the backbone of how users interact with an API. They define the path through which different resources and data are accessed, as well as the operations performed on those resources.

What is an Endpoint?

An API endpoint refers to a specific URL where an API can access a resource or provide functionality. It's the combination of a URL and the specific action that can be taken. The API endpoint is what developers target when they send requests to an API.

Example:

If an API has an endpoint like /api/users/123, this URL might be used to fetch details about the user with ID 123. Here, /users/123 is the resource, and the action taken (like fetching or deleting) depends on the HTTP method used.

What is a Route?

Routes define how URLs (or URIs) map to functionality in the server. A route usually consists of the URL pattern and the handler function that gets executed when that pattern is matched. In the context of Flask, routes are defined using Python decorators and specify what happens when a certain URL is requested.

Example in Flask:

```python
Copy code
@app.route('/api/users/<int:user_id>', methods=['GET'])
def get_user(user_id):
    return jsonify({'user': user_id})
```

In this example, /api/users/<user_id> is the route, and the get_user function handles requests sent to that route. The part <int:user_id> is a dynamic URL component that allows fetching a specific user based on their ID.

Defining Resources via Routes and Endpoints

Each resource in an API is accessed via specific routes or endpoints. For example, you might have the following API endpoints for a user resource:

- GET /api/users – Fetch all users.
- POST /api/users – Create a new user.
- GET /api/users/<id> – Fetch details for a specific user.
- PUT /api/users/<id> – Update details of a specific user.
- DELETE /api/users/<id> – Delete a specific user.

1.4 Key Concepts: HTTP Methods and Status Codes

APIs rely on HTTP methods to define the types of actions that can be taken on resources. Each HTTP method serves a distinct purpose and is used in different scenarios.

CHAPTER 1: INTRODUCTION TO API DEVELOPMENT

HTTP Methods

1. **GET**

- Purpose: Retrieve data from the server.
- Example: Fetching a list of users or the details of a specific user.
- Non-Idempotent Example: None, since GET requests are idempotent, meaning making the same request multiple times will yield the same result.

1. **POST**

- Purpose: Submit data to the server, often creating a new resource.
- Example: Submitting a new user registration form.
- Non-Idempotent Example: Creating a new user each time the request is sent.

1. **PUT**

- Purpose: Update an existing resource or create it if it does not exist.
- Example: Updating a user's profile information.
- Non-Idempotent Example: Updating the same user multiple times with the same data yields the same result.

1. **DELETE**

- Purpose: Remove a resource from the server.
- Example: Deleting a user's account.
- Non-Idempotent Example: Deleting a user once or multiple times produces the same effect (user no longer exists).

1. **PATCH**

- Purpose: Partially update a resource.
- Example: Changing a user's email address without affecting other profile details.
- Non-Idempotent Example: Multiple PATCH requests to update the email will produce the same result if the request is identical.

HTTP Status Codes

HTTP status codes are three-digit numbers that indicate the outcome of an API request. They provide information about whether the request was successful, encountered an error, or resulted in a redirection. Status codes are grouped into categories based on their first digit:

- **2xx Success**: Indicates that the request was successful.
- 200 OK: The request was successful, and the server returned the requested data.
- 201 Created: The request was successful, and a new resource was created.
- 204 No Content: The request was successful, but there is no content to return.
- **3xx Redirection**: Indicates that further action needs to be taken by the client.
- 301 Moved Permanently: The resource has been moved to a new location permanently.
- 302 Found: The resource has been temporarily moved to a new location.
- **4xx Client Errors**: Indicates an error caused by the client's request.
- 400 Bad Request: The request was malformed or invalid.
- 401 Unauthorized: Authentication is required to access the resource.
- 403 Forbidden: The client does not have permission to access the resource.
- 404 Not Found: The requested resource could not be found on the server.
- **5xx Server Errors**: Indicates an error on the server's side.
- 500 Internal Server Error: An unexpected error occurred on the server.
- 503 Service Unavailable: The server is currently unable to handle the request.

1.5 Overview of the Flask Framework for API Development

Flask is a micro-framework for Python that is commonly used to build web applications and APIs. It is lightweight, flexible, and easy to extend, making it a popular choice for developers who need to build simple APIs quickly without unnecessary overhead. Flask provides a simple and intuitive interface to develop powerful APIs with minimal boilerplate code.

Why Use Flask for API Development?

1. **Lightweight**: Flask is designed to be lightweight, giving developers control over what libraries and modules to use. It does not come with unnecessary features or functionalities, which makes it ideal for small to medium-sized applications or APIs.
2. **Flexible and Extensible**: Flask can easily be extended with libraries and plugins, allowing developers to add features like database connectivity, authentication, and more.
3. **Easy to Learn**: Flask's simple and minimalistic approach makes it easy for beginners to get started with API development.
4. **Strong Community and Documentation**: Flask has a large, active community, and excellent documentation, making it easy to find tutorials, guides, and solutions to common problems.

Flask for API Development: Basic Features

- **Routing**: Flask makes it easy to define API endpoints with flexible routing options.
- **Request and Response Handling**: Flask provides tools to handle HTTP requests, parse JSON data, and send responses.
- **Middleware Support**: Flask supports adding middleware for tasks such as logging, authentication, and data validation.
- **Integration with Other Libraries**: Flask integrates well with SQLAlchemy for database management, Flask-JWT for authentication, and Flask-CORS for enabling cross-origin resource sharing.

Chapter 2: Setting Up Flask for API Development

Before diving into API development with Flask, you need to set up the necessary environment and understand the structure of a Flask application. Flask is a minimal framework, meaning it provides flexibility and simplicity while allowing you to build complex APIs with additional libraries as needed. This chapter will guide you through installing Flask, setting up a virtual environment, building your first Flask API, and debugging your application.

2.1 Installing Flask and Virtual Environments

The first step in building Flask APIs is setting up your development environment. Using a virtual environment is recommended, as it allows you to manage project-specific dependencies without interfering with your system-wide Python packages.

Why Use Virtual Environments?

A virtual environment helps you manage dependencies on a per-project basis. For example, if one of your projects relies on Flask version 1.x and another project uses Flask version 2.x, you can isolate these dependencies within their respective virtual environments. This ensures there are no conflicts when working on different projects.

Setting Up a Virtual Environment

CHAPTER 2: SETTING UP FLASK FOR API DEVELOPMENT

1. **Install Python**: Ensure Python is installed on your machine. Flask works with Python 3.x, so check the version using:

```bash
Copy code
python --version
```

1. **Install virtualenv**: The virtualenv package allows you to create isolated environments. You can install it using pip:

```bash
Copy code
pip install virtualenv
```

1. **Create a Virtual Environment**: Navigate to your project directory and create a virtual environment:

```bash
Copy code
mkdir flask_api_project
cd flask_api_project
python -m venv venv
```

1. Here, venv is the name of the virtual environment folder.
2. **Activate the Virtual Environment**:

- On Windows:

```bash
Copy code
venv\Scripts\activate
```

- On macOS/Linux:

```bash
Copy code
source venv/bin/activate
```

1. Once activated, the terminal prompt will indicate that the environment is active (e.g., (venv) at the start of the prompt).
2. **Install Flask**: After activating your virtual environment, install Flask:

```bash
Copy code
pip install Flask
```

1. Flask should now be installed within your virtual environment.
2. **Freezing Dependencies**: Once you install additional dependencies, you can save them in a requirements.txt file, which makes it easier to recreate the environment:

```bash
Copy code
```

```
pip freeze > requirements.txt
```

1. This file can be used to install the same dependencies in another environment using:

```bash
Copy code
pip install -r requirements.txt
```

Deactivating the Virtual Environment

When you're done working on the project, you can deactivate the virtual environment:

```bash
Copy code
deactivate
```

2.2 Flask App Structure for APIs

Flask applications are flexible in how they are structured, but following a clean, consistent structure is essential for scalability and maintainability. Here's a simple structure that works well for Flask API development:

```arduino
Copy code
flask_api_project/
    app/
        __init__.py
        routes.py
        models.py
        utils.py
```

```
tests/      ├─────
    test_api.py  ├──────

venv/    ├─────

config.py  ├─────
run.py    └─────
requirements.txt
```

Explanation of the Structure:

- **app/**: This directory contains the main application files.
- **__init__.py**: This file initializes the Flask app and imports necessary configurations and routes.
- **routes.py**: This file defines the API endpoints and their functionality.
- **models.py**: This file defines your database models (if applicable).
- **utils.py**: This file includes utility functions that are used across the application.
- **tests/**: This directory contains the test files for your API.
- **venv/**: This directory holds your virtual environment files.
- **config.py**: This file stores configuration settings, such as environment variables, database URLs, or API keys.
- **run.py**: This script is the entry point of your Flask application. It contains code to run the Flask server.
- **requirements.txt**: This file lists the dependencies required by your application.

Creating Your First Flask App Structure

Let's go ahead and create a simple structure. Start by creating an app directory and some files inside it:

CHAPTER 2: SETTING UP FLASK FOR API DEVELOPMENT

```bash
Copy code
mkdir app
touch app/__init__.py app/routes.py app/models.py app/utils.py
touch config.py run.py
```

Now, you can initialize your Flask app in the app/__init__.py file:

```python
Copy code
from flask import Flask

def create_app():
    app = Flask(__name__)

    # Register routes from routes.py
    from .routes import api_routes
    app.register_blueprint(api_routes)

    return app
```

In the routes.py file, define your first route:

```python
Copy code
from flask import Blueprint, jsonify

api_routes = Blueprint('api_routes', __name__)

@api_routes.route('/api/hello', methods=['GET'])
def hello_world():
    return jsonify({'message': 'Hello, World!'})
```

Finally, in the run.py file, add the code to run the Flask server:

```python
Copy code
from app import create_app

app = create_app()

if __name__ == '__main__':
    app.run(debug=True)
```

This basic structure will allow your application to grow as you add more features.

2.3 Basic Flask API: Your First Endpoint

Once you have your project set up, it's time to create your first API endpoint. In this section, we will walk through creating a simple GET endpoint that returns a JSON response.

Step-by-Step: Creating Your First Endpoint

1. **Define the Route**: Open app/routes.py and define an endpoint:

```python
Copy code
from flask import Blueprint, jsonify

api_routes = Blueprint('api_routes', __name__)

@api_routes.route('/api/greet/<name>', methods=['GET'])
def greet_user(name):
    return jsonify({'message': f'Hello, {name}!'})
```

1. This route accepts a dynamic name parameter, which gets passed to the function and is returned in the JSON response.
2. **Run the Flask App**: Now, open run.py and ensure your Flask app is set to run:

CHAPTER 2: SETTING UP FLASK FOR API DEVELOPMENT

```python
Copy code
from app import create_app

app = create_app()

if __name__ == '__main__':
    app.run(debug=True)
```

1. **Start the Application**: In your terminal, run the application using:

```bash
Copy code
python run.py
```

1. **Access the Endpoint**: In your browser or API testing tool (like Postman or Curl), navigate to http://127.0.0.1:5000/api/greet/John. You should see a response like:

```json
Copy code
{
  "message": "Hello, John!"
}
```

Congratulations! You have just created your first Flask API endpoint that dynamically responds to the user input.

Working with Different HTTP Methods

Flask allows you to define routes that respond to different HTTP methods, such as POST, PUT, and DELETE. Let's add another route that handles a

POST request:

```python
Copy code
@api_routes.route('/api/data', methods=['POST'])
def receive_data():
    data = request.json  # Access JSON data sent in the request
    return jsonify({'received_data': data}), 201
```

This route listens for a POST request and echoes back the JSON data that was sent to it. If you use a tool like Postman, you can send JSON data to this endpoint and see the response.

2.4 Flask Debugging Tools

Debugging is an essential part of development, and Flask provides several useful tools to help developers identify and fix issues quickly.

Flask's Built-in Debugger

Flask comes with a built-in debugger that provides detailed error pages and allows you to inspect the state of your application at the point where an exception was raised.

To enable the debugger, set debug=True when running the app:

```python
Copy code
if __name__ == '__main__':
    app.run(debug=True)
```

When enabled, if an error occurs in your application, Flask will show a detailed traceback in the browser, including the specific line where the error occurred. You can also inspect the values of variables at that point.

Flask Shell

The Flask shell is an interactive Python shell that can be loaded with the application context. It is useful for testing, debugging, and interacting with your app's data directly. You can launch the Flask shell by running:

```bash
Copy code
flask shell
```

In the shell, you can interact with your Flask app, query the database, or test individual functions.

Debugging with pdb

Python's pdb (Python Debugger) can be used to pause the execution of your program and inspect its current state. You can insert a pdb breakpoint into your Flask app by adding the following line at the point where you want to pause the execution:

```python
Copy code
import pdb; pdb.set_trace()
```

When the code execution reaches this point, it will stop, and you can examine variables, step through code, or troubleshoot the issue interactively.

Logging Errors

Flask supports logging errors to keep track of what's happening in your application. By default, Flask logs errors to the console, but you can configure it to log errors to a file:

```python
Copy code
import logging
from logging.handlers import RotatingFileHandler

if not app.debug:
    file_handler = RotatingFileHandler('error.log',
    maxBytes=10240, backupCount=10)
    file_handler.setLevel(logging.ERROR)
    app.logger.addHandler(file_handler)
```

This setup logs errors to a file named error.log and ensures the log file does not grow too large by rotating it after reaching 10KB.

Chapter 3: Understanding Flask Routing and Views

Routing and views are foundational components of a Flask application, particularly in API development. The route defines the URL path and HTTP methods that trigger specific functions (views) in your application. Views then handle incoming requests and return appropriate responses, which could be JSON for APIs or HTML for web apps. In this chapter, we will explore how to define routes, work with URL variables and query parameters, handle various HTTP methods (GET and POST), and structure responses in Flask.

3.1 Defining Routes and Views in Flask

A **route** in Flask maps a URL to a Python function (also called a view). Whenever a request is made to a specific URL, Flask determines which view should handle the request based on the defined route.

Creating a Basic Route

In Flask, routes are defined using the @app.route() decorator. Here's an example of a simple route that handles a GET request:

```python
Copy code
from flask import Flask

app = Flask(__name__)

@app.route('/')
def index():
    return "Welcome to the Flask API!"
```

In this example:

- @app.route('/') maps the root URL (/) to the index function.
- The index function returns a simple string response ("Welcome to the Flask API!").

Handling Multiple Routes

Flask allows you to define multiple routes that trigger different functions based on the URL path. For example:

```python
Copy code
@app.route('/about')
def about():
    return "This is the about page."

@app.route('/contact')
def contact():
    return "Contact us at: contact@example.com"
```

Now, the /about URL will return the about page, and /contact will return the contact details.

Specifying HTTP Methods for Routes

By default, routes handle only GET requests. However, you can specify other HTTP methods (such as POST, PUT, and DELETE) by passing the methods argument to the @app.route() decorator. For example:

```python
Copy code
@app.route('/submit', methods=['POST'])
def submit_form():
    return "Form submitted!"
```

Here, the /submit route only accepts POST requests. If you try to access this route using GET, Flask will return a 405 Method Not Allowed error.

Using Flask Blueprints

As your API grows, it becomes harder to manage routes within a single file. Flask provides **blueprints** to organize routes across multiple files. A blueprint allows you to define routes in separate modules, which can then be registered to the main app.

Example:

1. **Define a blueprint in routes.py:**

```python
Copy code
from flask import Blueprint

api_routes = Blueprint('api_routes', __name__)

@api_routes.route('/api/hello')
def hello():
    return "Hello, from the API!"
```

1. **Register the blueprint in your main application in app.py:**

```python
Copy code
from flask import Flask
from routes import api_routes

app = Flask(__name__)
app.register_blueprint(api_routes)

if __name__ == '__main__':
    app.run(debug=True)
```

With blueprints, you can maintain a clean and modular codebase by organizing routes into logical groupings.

3.2 URL Variables and Query Parameters

Dynamic URLs are essential for any API. Flask makes it easy to work with URL variables and query parameters, allowing your routes to respond to different inputs dynamically.

Using URL Variables

You can define routes with dynamic components (variables) by placing parts of the URL inside angle brackets (< >). Flask captures these variables and passes them to the corresponding view function.

Example:

```python
Copy code
@app.route('/user/<username>')
def show_user_profile(username):
    return f"User: {username}"
```

Here, <username> is a URL variable. When a request is made to /user/john, Flask passes john as the username argument to the show_user_profile function. The response would be: "User: john".

You can also specify types for URL variables. The most common types are:

- int: Accepts only integers.

CHAPTER 3: UNDERSTANDING FLASK ROUTING AND VIEWS

- float: Accepts floating-point numbers.
- path: Accepts a string with slashes.

Example with a type:

```python
Copy code
@app.route('/user/<int:user_id>')
def show_user_by_id(user_id):
    return f"User ID: {user_id}"
```

In this case, the route /user/123 would accept 123 as an integer. If a string like /user/john is passed, Flask will return a 404 Not Found error since john is not an integer.

Query Parameters

Query parameters are another way to pass dynamic data to a route. They appear after the ? symbol in the URL and are commonly used for filtering or pagination in APIs.

Example:

```python
Copy code
@app.route('/search')
def search():
    query = request.args.get('q')  # Get the 'q' parameter from
    the query string
    return f"Search query: {query}"
```

If you make a request to /search?q=flask, Flask retrieves the q parameter from the URL and returns the value "flask". If the q parameter is not provided, request.args.get('q') will return None.

Query parameters are flexible because you can add multiple parameters to the URL:

- /search?q=flask&page=2&limit=10

3.3 Handling GET and POST Requests

In API development, you'll frequently need to handle both GET and POST requests. GET is used to retrieve data, while POST is used to send data to the server.

Handling GET Requests

GET requests are used when the client wants to retrieve data from the server. For example, to fetch a list of users, you could define a route like this:

```python
Copy code
@app.route('/api/users', methods=['GET'])
def get_users():
    users = ["John", "Jane", "Doe"]
    return jsonify(users)
```

Here, the /api/users route responds to GET requests by returning a list of users in JSON format.

Handling POST Requests

POST requests are used to send data to the server, often when creating a new resource. Flask allows you to easily handle POST requests and access the sent data.

Example:

```python
Copy code
from flask import request

@app.route('/api/users', methods=['POST'])
def create_user():
    data = request.json  # Access the JSON data sent in the request
    username = data.get('username')
    return jsonify({'message': f'User {username} created!'}), 201
```

In this example:

CHAPTER 3: UNDERSTANDING FLASK ROUTING AND VIEWS

- The client sends a POST request to /api/users with a JSON body (e.g., {"username": "john"}).
- Flask accesses the JSON data using request.json and retrieves the username field.
- A success message is returned, and the 201 Created status code is sent to indicate that a new resource has been created.

Validating Request Data

When handling POST requests, it's essential to validate the incoming data to ensure the correct format. For instance, you might want to check that the username field is present:

```python
Copy code
@app.route('/api/users', methods=['POST'])
def create_user():
    data = request.json
    if 'username' not in data:
        return jsonify({'error': 'Username is required'}), 400
    username = data['username']
    return jsonify({'message':
f'User {username} created!'}), 201
```

If the username field is missing from the request, Flask returns a 400 Bad Request error with an appropriate message.

3.4 Structuring Responses: JSON and HTML

Flask supports multiple response formats, including JSON (commonly used in APIs) and HTML (used in web apps). Structuring your responses properly ensures that the client receives data in the expected format.

Returning JSON Responses

For APIs, JSON is the most commonly used format. Flask makes it easy to return JSON using the jsonify() function, which serializes Python objects into JSON format and sets the appropriate Content-Type header.

Example:

```python
Copy code
from flask import jsonify

@app.route('/api/user/<int:user_id>',
 methods=['GET'])
def get_user(user_id):
    user = {'id': user_id, 'name': 'John Doe'}
    return jsonify(user)
```

The jsonify() function converts the user dictionary to JSON and returns it as a response. The output would look like this:

```json
Copy code
{
  "id": 1,
  "name": "John Doe"
}
```

Flask automatically sets the Content-Type header to application/json.

Returning HTML Responses

While Flask APIs typically return JSON, Flask also allows you to return HTML for web-based responses. For example, a simple HTML response might look like this:

```python
Copy code
@app.route('/hello')
def hello_html():
    return "<h1>Hello, World!</h1>"
```

Flask also supports rendering HTML templates, which are useful for more complex web applications. Templates allow you to separate the logic of your application from the presentation layer (HTML). You can use the render_template() function to serve HTML templates:

```python
Copy code
from flask import render_template

@app.route('/greet/<name>')
def greet(name):
    return render_template
('greet.html', name=name)
```

In the templates/greet.html file:

```html
Copy code
<!DOCTYPE html>
<html>
<head>
    <title>Greet User</title>
</head>
<body>
    <h1>Hello, {{ name }}!</h1>
</body>
</html>
```

When the route /greet/John is accessed, Flask renders the greet.html template and passes the name variable to it, resulting in an HTML page that says "Hello, John!".

Chapter 4: Flask Request and Response Cycle

Understanding how Flask processes requests and returns responses is crucial in API development. Flask follows a clear request-response cycle, where it handles incoming client requests, processes the data, and returns a response. In this chapter, we will explore the anatomy of a Flask request, examine the Request and Response objects, and learn how to return JSON responses and customize response codes and headers.

4.1 The Anatomy of a Flask Request

When a client sends an HTTP request to a Flask server, the server processes that request through several stages before returning a response. Here's an overview of the typical request-response cycle:

1. **Client Sends a Request**: The client (browser, mobile app, or API consumer) sends a request to the Flask server. The request contains data such as the URL, HTTP method, headers, and possibly a body (for POST or PUT requests).
2. **Flask Receives the Request**: Flask receives the request and examines the URL to determine which route matches. Based on the route and the HTTP method, Flask calls the corresponding view function.
3. **Request Object is Created**: A Request object is created that encapsu-

lates all the information from the incoming request (e.g., headers, URL parameters, JSON body).
4. **Processing the Request**: The view function processes the request. It can extract data from the Request object, query a database, perform calculations, or interact with other services.
5. **Response is Returned**: After processing the request, the view function returns a Response object. This can contain data in JSON, HTML, or other formats, and can also include custom headers and status codes.
6. **Flask Sends the Response**: Flask sends the Response object back to the client, completing the cycle.

4.2 Flask Request Object

The Request object in Flask provides access to all the data related to an incoming client request. You can access the Request object via the flask.request module.

Common Properties of the Request Object

Here are some important attributes of the Request object:

- **request.method**: Returns the HTTP method used in the request (e.g., GET, POST, PUT, DELETE).
- Example:

```python
Copy code
if request.method == 'POST':
    # Handle POST request
```

- **request.args**: Contains query parameters sent in the URL.
- Example:

```python
Copy code
search_query = request.args.get('q')
```

- If the client makes a request like /search?q=flask, the q parameter is retrieved using request.args.
- **request.form**: Contains form data sent in a POST request (usually from an HTML form).
- Example:

```python
Copy code
username = request.form.get('username')
```

- **request.json**: Contains the parsed JSON data from the request body if the client sent a JSON payload.
- Example:

```python
Copy code
data = request.json
email = data.get('email')
```

- **request.headers**: Returns the HTTP headers sent with the request.
- Example:

```python
Copy code
user_agent = request.headers.get('User-Agent')
```

- **request.files**: Provides access to files uploaded via a POST request (used for handling file uploads).
- Example:

```python
Copy code
uploaded_file = request.files['file']
```

Example of Accessing Request Data

Let's take an example where we want to handle a POST request that sends JSON data to create a new user:

```python
Copy code
from flask import request, jsonify

@app.route('/api/users', methods=['POST'])
def create_user():
    # Access JSON data
    data = request.json
    username = data.get('username')
    email = data.get('email')

    # Process and return a response
    return jsonify({'message': f'User {username} created with email {email}'}), 201
```

In this example:

- request.json is used to access the JSON body sent in the request.

- The JSON fields username and email are extracted from the data.

4.3 Flask Response Object

The Response object represents the server's response to a client request. Flask automatically generates a Response object when you return a string, a dictionary (which is converted to JSON), or an HTML page. However, you can manually create and customize a Response object if needed.

Common Ways to Return Responses

1. **Returning a String**: When you return a string from a view function, Flask automatically wraps it in a Response object with a status code of 200 OK.
2. Example:

```
python
Copy code
@app.route('/hello')
def hello():
    return "Hello, World!"
```

1. **Returning a Dictionary (JSON)**: Flask automatically converts dictionaries to JSON when you use jsonify(). This is common in APIs that return JSON responses.
2. Example:

```
python
Copy code
@app.route('/api/user')
def get_user():
    user_data = {'id': 1,
'name': 'John Doe'}
```

```
return jsonify(user_data)
```

1. **Manually Creating a Response**: You can manually create a Response object for more control over headers, status codes, or the response body.
2. Example:

```python
Copy code
from flask import Response

@app.route('/custom')
def custom_response():
    custom_data = '{"message": "This is a custom response."}'
    return Response(custom_data, status=200,
    mimetype='application/json')
```

Customizing the Response Object

You can customize the Response object by setting headers, status codes, and content types. Here's how you can create a response with custom headers:

```python
Copy code
@app.route('/custom_headers')
def custom_headers():
    response = jsonify({'message': 'Custom headers example'})
    response.headers['X-Custom-Header'] = 'CustomValue'
    return response
```

This example adds a custom header X-Custom-Header to the response.

4.4 Returning JSON Responses

APIs typically return data in JSON format because it is lightweight, human-readable, and easily parsed by most programming languages. Flask provides the jsonify() function to make returning JSON responses simple.

Using jsonify()

The jsonify() function converts a Python dictionary into a JSON string and sets the correct content type (application/json).

Example:

```python
from flask import jsonify

@app.route('/api/user/<int:user_id>',
 methods=['GET'])
def get_user(user_id):
    user = {
        'id': user_id,
        'name': 'John Doe',
        'email': 'john@example.com'
    }
    return jsonify(user)
```

In this example:

- The user data is returned as a JSON response.
- The jsonify() function handles the conversion of the Python dictionary to JSON.

JSON Response with Custom Status Codes

By default, jsonify() returns a 200 OK status code. You can specify a different status code by passing it as a second argument.

Example:

```python
@app.route('/api/create_user', methods=['POST'])
def create_user():
    data = request.json
    if not data.get('username'):
```

```
        return jsonify({'error': 'Username is required'}), 400
    # Process the data...
    return jsonify({'message':
'User created'}), 201
```

In this case:

- If the request is missing a username, the response will return a 400 Bad Request status.
- If the request is successful, a 201 Created status is returned.

4.5 Custom Response Codes and Headers

In some cases, you may need to return specific HTTP status codes or add custom headers to your response. Flask allows you to easily customize both status codes and headers in your responses.

Custom Status Codes

Flask provides flexibility in returning custom status codes. You can specify the status code either by returning it as part of a tuple or by setting it explicitly in the Response object.

Example with jsonify():

```
python
Copy code
@app.route('/api/resource', methods=['GET'])
def get_resource():
    data = {'message': 'Resource not found'}
    return jsonify(data), 404  # 404 Not Found
```

Example with Response object:

```
python
Copy code
from flask import Response
```

```
@app.route('/custom_code')
def custom_code():
    return Response("Custom status
 code", status=202)  # 202 Accepted
```

Custom Headers

To add custom headers to a response, you can modify the headers dictionary in the Response object.

Example:

```python
Copy code
@app.route('/custom_headers')
def custom_headers():
    response = jsonify({'message':
'Check the headers'})
    response.headers['X-App-Version'] =
'1.0.0'
    return response
```

In this example:

- The X-App-Version header is added to the response. When the client receives the response, they can check the custom header in the response headers.

Combining Status Codes and Headers

You can combine custom status codes and headers in a single response. For example:

```python
Copy code
@app.route('/combined')
def combined():
    response = jsonify({'message':
```

```
'Custom response with headers and status code'})
    response.status_code = 201
    response.headers['X-Custom-Header']
= 'HeaderValue'
    return response
```

This example returns a 201 Created status code and adds a custom header (X-Custom-Header) to the response.

Chapter 5: Database Integration with Flask

Most API-driven applications rely on databases to store, manage, and retrieve data. In this chapter, we will focus on integrating databases into Flask applications using SQLAlchemy, a popular Object-Relational Mapping (ORM) tool. We will cover setting up SQLAlchemy, creating database models, performing CRUD operations, and managing database migrations with Flask-Migrate.

5.1 Introduction to Databases in Flask

Flask, being a micro-framework, does not include built-in support for databases, but it easily integrates with popular database tools such as SQLAlchemy. Using an ORM like SQLAlchemy allows developers to interact with databases using Python code rather than writing raw SQL queries. SQLAlchemy abstracts the database layer, enabling you to define models (classes) that map to tables in your database.

Why Use SQLAlchemy?

- **Abstraction**: SQLAlchemy abstracts the database layer, allowing developers to work with Python objects rather than writing SQL queries manually.
- **Cross-Database Compatibility**: SQLAlchemy supports multiple databases (PostgreSQL, MySQL, SQLite, etc.) and allows for easy

switching between them.
- **Ease of Use**: SQLAlchemy's ORM functionality simplifies complex database operations, such as querying, joining tables, and managing relationships.
- **Scalability**: Using SQLAlchemy allows you to create scalable database-driven applications.

5.2 Setting Up SQLAlchemy for Flask APIs

To integrate SQLAlchemy with your Flask app, you first need to install the necessary packages and configure the database.

Step 1: Installing SQLAlchemy and Flask-SQLAlchemy

First, install the SQLAlchemy and Flask-SQLAlchemy packages using pip:

```bash
Copy code
pip install SQLAlchemy Flask-SQLAlchemy
```

Step 2: Configuring the Database in Flask

Next, configure your Flask app to use SQLAlchemy by setting up the database URI. You'll also need to initialize an instance of SQLAlchemy in your application.

1. **Define Configuration in config.py:**
2. Create a config.py file to store your database configuration:

```python
Copy code
import os

basedir = os.path.abspath(os.path.dirname(__file__))
```

```
class Config:
    SQLALCHEMY_DATABASE_URI = 'sqlite:///' + os.path.join(basedir,
    'app.db')
# SQLite as an example
    SQLALCHEMY_TRACK_MODIFICATIONS = False
```

1. This configuration connects your app to an SQLite database (app.db). For production, you might use other databases like PostgreSQL or MySQL.
2. **Initialize SQLAlchemy in app/__init__.py:**
3. In your app/__init__.py file, initialize the Flask app and set up SQLAlchemy:

```
python
Copy code
from flask import Flask
from flask_sqlalchemy import SQLAlchemy
from config import Config

db = SQLAlchemy()

def create_app():
    app = Flask(__name__)
    app.config.from_object(Config)

    db.init_app(app)

    return app
```

1. **Create the Database (Optional for SQLite):**
2. If you're using SQLite, the database file (app.db) will be automatically created when you run the application and define models. For other databases like PostgreSQL or MySQL, ensure that you create the database manually before running the application.

5.3 Creating Models and Tables

In SQLAlchemy, database tables are represented by Python classes known as **models**. Each model corresponds to a table in the database, and each attribute of the model corresponds to a column in that table.

Step 1: Defining a Model

Create a models.py file in the app/ directory where you'll define your models. Here's an example of a User model:

```python
Copy code
from app import db

class User(db.Model):
    __tablename__ = 'users'

    id = db.Column(db.Integer, primary_key=True)
    username = db.Column(db.String(64), unique=True, nullable=False)
    email = db.Column(db.String(120), unique=True, nullable=False)
    created_at = db.Column(db.DateTime, default=db.func.current_timestamp())

    def __repr__(self):
        return f'<User {self.username}>'
```

In this example:

- The User class defines a table called users.
- id, username, email, and created_at are columns in the users table.
- id is the primary key, which uniquely identifies each record.
- username and email are unique fields, ensuring that no two users can have the same username or email.
- created_at automatically records the timestamp when a new user is created.

Step 2: Creating Tables

After defining your models, you need to create the corresponding tables in the database. In Flask, you can create the tables using the following commands:

1. **Open a Python shell** in your project directory:

```bash
Copy code
flask shell
```

1. **Import the database instance and create the tables:**

```python
Copy code
from app import db
db.create_all()
```

1. This will generate the users table in your database (e.g., app.db for SQLite).

5.4 CRUD Operations with Flask and SQLAlchemy

CRUD (Create, Read, Update, Delete) operations are the essential building blocks for interacting with a database. Let's explore how to perform CRUD operations using SQLAlchemy in Flask.

Create: Adding Records to the Database

To create new records in the database, you create an instance of the model, set its attributes, and add it to the session. Finally, commit the session to save the record.

Example:

```python
Copy code
@app.route('/api/users', methods=['POST'])
def create_user():
    data = request.json
    new_user = User(username=data['username'], email=data['email'])

    db.session.add(new_user)
# Add the new user to the session
    db.session.commit()  # Commit
the transaction to save the user

    return jsonify({'message': 'User created successfully!'}), 201
```

In this example:

- A new User object is created using data from the request.
- The new user is added to the session using db.session.add().
- The session is committed to save the new record in the database.

Read: Retrieving Records from the Database

To retrieve records, you can use methods like User.query.all() (to get all users) or User.query.get(id) (to get a user by ID).

Example:

```python
Copy code
@app.route('/api/users', methods=['GET'])
def get_users():
    users = User.query.all()
    user_list = [{'id': user.id, 'username': user.username,
    'email': user.email}
for user in users]
    return jsonify(user_list)
```

In this example:

- User.query.all() fetches all records from the users table.
- The result is converted to a list of dictionaries and returned as a JSON response.

Update: Modifying Existing Records

To update a record, you first query it from the database, modify the necessary fields, and then commit the changes.

Example:

```python
Copy code
@app.route('/api/users/<int:user_id>', methods=['PUT'])
def update_user(user_id):
    user = User.query.get_or_404(user_id)
    data = request.json
    user.username = data['username']
    user.email = data['email']

    db.session.commit()  # Commit the changes to save the updated user

    return jsonify({'message': 'User updated successfully!'})
```

In this example:

- User.query.get_or_404(user_id) fetches the user by ID or returns a 404 error if the user is not found.
- The username and email fields are updated based on the request data.
- The session is committed to save the changes.

Delete: Removing Records from the Database

To delete a record, query it from the database, remove it using db.session.delete(), and commit the changes.

Example:

CHAPTER 5: DATABASE INTEGRATION WITH FLASK

```python
Copy code
@app.route('/api/users/<int:user_id>', methods=['DELETE'])
def delete_user(user_id):
    user = User.query.get_or_404(user_id)

    db.session.delete(user)
# Remove the user from the session
    db.session.commit()   #
Commit the transaction to delete the user

    return jsonify({'message': 'User deleted successfully!'})
```

In this example:

- The user is retrieved from the database.
- The user is deleted using db.session.delete().
- The session is committed to reflect the deletion in the database.

5.5 Database Migrations with Flask-Migrate

As your application evolves, the database schema may need to change (e.g., adding new columns, modifying existing ones). Flask-Migrate is an extension that simplifies database migrations using Alembic, a tool that handles database version control.

Step 1: Installing Flask-Migrate

Install Flask-Migrate using pip:

```bash
Copy code
pip install Flask-Migrate
```

Step 2: Initializing Flask-Migrate

In app/__init__.py, import Migrate and initialize it with the app and SQLAlchemy instance:

47

```python
Copy code
from flask_migrate import Migrate
from app import db

migrate = Migrate()

def create_app():
    app = Flask(__name__)
    app.config.from_object(Config)

    db.init_app(app)
    migrate.init_app(app, db)

    return app
```

Step 3: Creating Migration Scripts

Once Flask-Migrate is set up, you can create migration scripts to handle changes in the database schema.

1. **Initialize the migration repository:**
2. Run this command to set up the migration directory:

```bash
Copy code
flask db init
```

1. This will create a migrations/ directory in your project.
2. **Generate a migration script:**
3. When you make changes to your models (e.g., adding a new field), generate a migration script:

CHAPTER 5: DATABASE INTEGRATION WITH FLASK

```bash
Copy code
flask db migrate -m "Added new field to User model"
```

1. **Apply the migration to the database:**
2. After generating the migration script, apply the changes to the database:

```bash
Copy code
flask db upgrade
```

1. This will apply the migration and update the database schema accordingly.

Step 4: Managing Migrations

Flask-Migrate also provides commands for managing migrations:

- **flask db downgrade**: Reverts the last migration.
- **flask db history**: Shows the migration history.
- **flask db stamp**: Stamps the database with a specific revision without applying any changes.

Chapter 6: Handling Errors and Exceptions in Flask APIs

In API development, handling errors gracefully is crucial to ensure a good user experience and provide useful feedback to the client. Flask provides mechanisms to handle exceptions and errors in a structured way. This chapter will cover the basics of error handling in Flask, how to create custom error handlers for APIs, how to work with Flask's built-in HTTPException class, and how to log errors to aid in debugging and system monitoring.

6.1 Flask Error Handling Basics

Flask provides default error handling for common HTTP status codes, such as 404 Not Found and 500 Internal Server Error. When an error occurs in a Flask application, Flask automatically returns an appropriate HTTP response with a relevant status code. However, for APIs, it's essential to provide more structured, consistent error messages, especially when returning JSON responses.

Default Error Responses

By default, Flask returns simple HTML responses for common errors. For example:
- A 404 Not Found error occurs when a requested route does not exist.
- A 500 Internal Server Error occurs when there's an unhandled exception

CHAPTER 6: HANDLING ERRORS AND EXCEPTIONS IN FLASK APIS

in the application.

Example of a default 404 response:

```html
Copy code
<!DOCTYPE HTML PUBLIC "-//W3C//DTD HTML 3.2 Final//EN">
<title>404 Not Found</title>
<h1>Not Found</h1>
<p>The requested URL was not found on the server.</p>
```

For an API, this type of response is not suitable. Instead, you would want to return a structured JSON response with a useful error message.

Handling Errors with abort()

Flask provides the abort() function to manually trigger errors. This is useful when you want to enforce certain conditions or return specific error codes from within your API endpoints.

Example:

```python
Copy code
from flask import abort

@app.route('/api/resource/<int:id>')
def get_resource(id):
    if id < 1:
        abort(400, description="Invalid ID. Must be greater than 0.")

    # Fetch the resource from the database...
    return jsonify({'id': id, 'name': 'Resource Name'})
```

In this example, if the id is less than 1, a 400 Bad Request error is returned with a custom message.

6.2 Custom Error Handlers for APIs

For a consistent API experience, you should define custom error handlers that return JSON responses for different types of errors. Flask allows you to register custom error handlers using the errorhandler() decorator.

Creating a Custom Error Handler

You can create custom error handlers for specific status codes, such as 404 or 500, or even handle general exceptions.

Example: Handling a 404 Not Found error:

```python
Copy code
from flask import jsonify

@app.errorhandler(404)
def resource_not_found(error):
    return jsonify({'error':
 'Resource not found',
 'message': str(error)}), 404
```

Now, whenever a 404 error occurs, Flask will return a JSON response with a structured error message instead of the default HTML page.

Customizing Error Messages

You can extend the custom error handler to return more information, such as error codes, detailed messages, and possible resolutions.

Example: Handling a 400 Bad Request error:

```python
Copy code
@app.errorhandler(400)
def bad_request(error):
    return jsonify({
        'error': 'Bad Request',
        'message': str(error),
        'suggestion': 'Please
 verify your request and try again.'
    }), 400
```

By customizing error messages, you help clients understand what went wrong and how to fix their requests.

6.3 Flask HTTPException and Response Codes

Flask's HTTPException class provides a way to handle errors more flexibly. It serves as the base class for many built-in HTTP exceptions, and you can raise HTTPException with custom error codes and messages.

Using HTTPException

The abort() function can be used to raise an HTTPException with a specific status code and message.

Example:

```python
Copy code
from werkzeug.exceptions import HTTPException

@app.route('/api/items/<int:item_id>')
def get_item(item_id):
    if item_id > 100:
        abort(HTTPException(description="Item not found", code=404))
    return jsonify({'id': item_id, 'name': 'Item Name'})
```

In this example, if the item_id exceeds 100, a 404 Not Found error is triggered with a custom message.

Customizing HTTPException Responses

You can also subclass HTTPException to create custom exceptions with specific response structures.

Example: Creating a custom InvalidUsage exception:

```python
Copy code
from werkzeug.exceptions import HTTPException

class InvalidUsage(HTTPException):
    code = 400
```

```python
    description = "Invalid request"

    def __init__(self, message, code=None):
        HTTPException.__init__(self)
        self.message = message
        if code:
            self.code = code

    def get_body(self, environ=None):
        return jsonify({
            'error': 'Invalid Usage',
            'message': self.message
        }).get_data()

    def get_headers(self, environ=None):
        return [('Content-Type', 'application/json')]

@app.route('/api/data')
def process_data():
    raise InvalidUsage('This data is incorrect', code=422)
```

Here, we create a custom InvalidUsage exception that can be raised whenever there's an issue with the request. It returns a JSON response with a detailed message and a custom status code (in this case, 422).

6.4 Logging Errors in Flask APIs

Logging errors is crucial for debugging and monitoring the health of your application. By logging errors, you can capture important information when exceptions occur and analyze them later to identify and resolve issues.

Setting Up Logging in Flask

Flask uses Python's built-in logging module to handle logging. You can configure Flask to log errors to a file for further analysis.

Example: Setting up a basic error log:

```
python
Copy code
```

CHAPTER 6: HANDLING ERRORS AND EXCEPTIONS IN FLASK APIS

```python
import logging
from logging.handlers import RotatingFileHandler

if not app.debug:
    # Create a file handler that logs error messages
    file_handler = RotatingFileHandler('error.log',
    maxBytes=10240, backupCount=10)
    file_handler.setLevel(logging.ERROR)

    # Add the handler to the Flask app logger
    app.logger.addHandler(file_handler)
```

In this example:

- The RotatingFileHandler ensures that the log file size is limited to 10KB, and up to 10 backup log files are kept.
- Only error messages (logging.ERROR) are logged.
- Errors are written to error.log.

Logging Exceptions

You can use Flask's built-in logging system to log exceptions whenever they occur. Flask's logger object captures unhandled exceptions, which are useful for debugging.

Example: Logging exceptions in custom error handlers:

```
python
Copy code
@app.errorhandler(500)
def internal_server_error(error):
    app.logger.error(f'Server Error: {error}, Route: {request.url}')
    return jsonify({'error': 'Internal Server Error'}), 500
```

In this example:

- When a 500 Internal Server Error occurs, the error message and the URL of the failed request are logged.
- This log data helps track issues in specific routes and requests.

External Logging Tools

For more advanced logging, consider integrating external logging services such as **Sentry, Loggly,** or **Elastic Stack (ELK)**. These tools provide more powerful logging, monitoring, and alerting features.

Example: Integrating Sentry for error logging:

```bash
Copy code
pip install sentry-sdk
```

```python
Copy code
import sentry_sdk
from sentry_sdk.integrations.flask import FlaskIntegration

sentry_sdk.init(
    dsn="YOUR_SENTRY_DSN",
    integrations=[FlaskIntegration()]
)
```

Sentry will automatically capture unhandled exceptions, and you can track them on Sentry's dashboard in real time.

Chapter 7: Authentication and Authorization in Flask APIs

Security is a critical aspect of API development, ensuring that only authorized users have access to specific resources or functionalities. This chapter focuses on different methods to secure Flask APIs, including basic authentication, token-based authentication using JSON Web Tokens (JWT), OAuth2 for third-party integrations, and securing endpoints using Flask-HTTPAuth.

7.1 Introduction to API Security

APIs expose data and services to clients, which makes them attractive targets for attacks. Therefore, ensuring the security of your API is crucial to prevent unauthorized access, data breaches, and other security threats.

There are two key concepts in API security:

1. **Authentication**: Verifying the identity of a user or client attempting to access the API. This ensures that the person or system making the request is who they claim to be.
2. **Authorization**: Once authenticated, determining what resources or actions the user is allowed to access. This ensures that even authenticated users cannot access resources or perform actions they do not have permission for.

Common API Security Approaches:

- **Basic Authentication**: A simple, yet insecure method of sending credentials (username and password) with each request.
- **Token-Based Authentication**: A more secure method where clients are issued tokens (such as JWT) after authentication, which are used to authenticate subsequent requests.
- **OAuth2**: A widely used authorization framework that allows secure access to resources from third-party services without exposing user credentials.

7.2 Implementing Basic Authentication

Basic Authentication is the simplest form of authentication in which the client sends the username and password in the Authorization header of each request. Although it is easy to implement, it is not recommended for production environments without encryption (such as HTTPS) due to its inherent insecurity.

Example: Implementing Basic Authentication in Flask

Flask-HTTPAuth is a helpful library to implement basic authentication in Flask applications.

Step 1: Install Flask-HTTPAuth:

```bash
Copy code
pip install Flask-HTTPAuth
```

Step 2: Implement Basic Authentication:

```python
Copy code
from flask import Flask, jsonify
from flask_httpauth import HTTPBasicAuth
```

CHAPTER 7: AUTHENTICATION AND AUTHORIZATION IN FLASK APIS

```python
app = Flask(__name__)
auth = HTTPBasicAuth()

# Mock user data
users = {
    "john": "hello123",
    "admin": "secret"
}

@auth.verify_password
def verify_password(username, password):
    if username in users and users[username] == password:
        return username
    return None

@app.route('/api/protected')
@auth.login_required
def get_protected_data():
    return jsonify({'message': f'Hello, {auth.current_user()}! This is protected data.'})

if __name__ == '__main__':
    app.run(debug=True)
```

In this example:

- **@auth.verify_password**: This function is used to verify the credentials by checking the username and password against the mock user data.
- **@auth.login_required**: This decorator ensures that the endpoint is protected and accessible only to authenticated users.
- The client must send a valid Authorization header in the format Basic base64(username:password).

Testing the API with Curl:

```bash
Copy code
curl -u john:hello123 http://127.0.0.1:5000/api/protected
```

This request will succeed and return a response because the correct username and password are provided.

Limitations of Basic Authentication:

- **Insecure**: Username and password are sent with every request, and without encryption (e.g., HTTPS), this can be intercepted by attackers.
- **No Session Management**: Credentials must be sent with every request, leading to inefficiency.

7.3 Token-Based Authentication (JWT)

Token-Based Authentication solves the issues of Basic Authentication by issuing a token upon successful authentication. This token is then sent with each request, eliminating the need to send credentials repeatedly. JSON Web Tokens (JWT) are commonly used for token-based authentication.

How JWT Works:

1. The user provides their credentials (username and password).
2. The server verifies the credentials and issues a JWT.
3. The client sends the JWT with every subsequent request in the Authorization header.
4. The server verifies the token to authorize access.

JWT Structure:

A JWT consists of three parts, separated by dots:

- **Header**: Contains the type of token (JWT) and the signing algorithm.
- **Payload**: Contains the claims, such as the user information and token expiration.
- **Signature**: A cryptographic signature to ensure the token's integrity.

CHAPTER 7: AUTHENTICATION AND AUTHORIZATION IN FLASK APIS

Example: Implementing JWT in Flask
Step 1: Install PyJWT:

```bash
Copy code
pip install PyJWT Flask-JWT-Extended
```

Step 2: Implement JWT Authentication:

```python
Copy code
from flask import Flask, jsonify, request
from flask_jwt_extended import JWTManager, create_access_token, jwt_required, get_jwt_identity

app = Flask(__name__)
app.config['JWT_SECRET_KEY'] = 'your_jwt_secret_key'  # Set a secret key for JWT
jwt = JWTManager(app)

users = {
    "john": "hello123"
}

@app.route('/api/login', methods=['POST'])
def login():
    username = request.json.get('username')
    password = request.json.get('password')

    if username in users and users[username] == password:
        token = create_access_token(identity=username)
        return jsonify({'access_token': token})

    return jsonify({'error': 'Invalid credentials'}), 401

@app.route('/api/protected', methods=['GET'])
@jwt_required()
def protected():
```

```
    current_user = get_jwt_identity()
    return jsonify({'message': f'Hello, {current_user}. This is
    protected data.'})

if __name__ == '__main__':
    app.run(debug=True)
```

In this example:

- The /api/login route verifies the user credentials and issues a JWT.
- The create_access_token() function generates the token, which is sent back to the client.
- The /api/protected route is protected by the @jwt_required() decorator, which ensures that the client sends a valid JWT with the request.
- The get_jwt_identity() function retrieves the identity of the user from the token.

Testing the API with Curl:

1. Log in to get a token:

bash
Copy code
```
curl -X POST -H "Content-Type: application/json" -d
'{"username":"john", "password":"hello123"}'
http://127.0.0.1:5000/api/login
```

1. Use the token to access the protected route:

bash
Copy code

```
curl -H "Authorization: Bearer <your_jwt_token>"
http://127.0.0.1:5000/api/protected
```

Advantages of JWT:

- **Stateless**: No need to store session data on the server.
- **Secure**: JWTs are signed, ensuring their integrity.
- **Efficiency**: Tokens can be easily passed between services without querying the database.

7.4 OAuth2 and Third-Party Integrations

OAuth2 is a protocol that allows third-party services to access a user's resources without exposing the user's credentials. OAuth2 is widely used for social login systems (e.g., logging in with Google or Facebook) and delegating access to APIs.

OAuth2 Flow:

1. **Authorization Request**: The user is redirected to the OAuth provider (e.g., Google) to log in.
2. **Authorization Grant**: The provider grants an authorization code to the client.
3. **Token Exchange**: The client exchanges the authorization code for an access token.
4. **Access Resource**: The client uses the access token to access the protected resources on behalf of the user.

Example: OAuth2 with Flask-Dance for Google Login

Flask-Dance is a library that makes it easy to integrate third-party OAuth services with Flask.

Step 1: Install Flask-Dance and OAuthlib:

```bash
Copy code
pip install Flask-Dance oauthlib
```

Step 2: Set up OAuth for Google Login:

```python
Copy code
from flask import Flask, redirect, url_for
from flask_dance.contrib.google import make_google_blueprint, google

app = Flask(__name__)
app.secret_key = 'your_secret_key'

# Set up the Google OAuth2 blueprint
google_bp = make_google_blueprint(client_id="your_google_client_id",
                                   client_secret="your_google_client_secret",
                                   redirect_to="google_login")
app.register_blueprint(google_bp, url_prefix="/login")

@app.route('/')
def index():
    return 'Welcome to the Flask OAuth2 Example!'

@app.route('/login/google')
def google_login():
    if not google.authorized:
        return redirect(url_for("google.login"))

    resp = google.
```

CHAPTER 7: AUTHENTICATION AND AUTHORIZATION IN FLASK APIS

```
get("/plus/v1/people/me")
assert resp.ok, resp.text
return f'You are
logged in as {resp.
json()["displayName"]}!'

if __name__ == '__main__':
    app.run(debug=True)
```

In this example:

- The **Flask-Dance** blueprint is used to handle Google OAuth2 login.
- When the user accesses /login/google, they are redirected to the Google login page. Once authenticated, the app retrieves the user profile using the Google API.

7.5 Securing API Endpoints with Flask-HTTPAuth

For further control over securing API endpoints, **Flask-HTTPAuth** can be used to implement authentication schemes, including basic, digest, and token authentication.

Example: Securing Endpoints with Token Authentication

In this example, we will implement token-based authentication using Flask-HTTPAuth.

```python
Copy code
from flask import Flask, jsonify
from flask_httpauth import HTTPTokenAuth

app = Flask(__name__)
auth = HTTPTokenAuth(scheme='Bearer')

# Mock tokens for demonstration purposes
tokens = {
    "token123": "john",
```

```python
    "token456": "admin"
}

@auth.verify_token
def verify_token(token):
    if token in tokens:
        return tokens[token]
    return None

@app.route('/api/secure-data')
@auth.login_required
def secure_data():
    return jsonify({'message': f'Hello, {auth.current_user()}! You have accessed secure data.'})

if __name__ == '__main__':
    app.run(debug=True)
```

In this example:

- **@auth.verify_token**: Verifies the token sent by the client.
- **@auth.login_required**: Ensures that the endpoint is protected and accessible only to users with valid tokens.

Testing the API with Curl:

```bash
Copy code
curl -H "Authorization: Bearer token123" http://127.0.0.1:5000/api/secure-data
```

Chapter 8: Building a RESTful API with Flask

REST (Representational State Transfer) is an architectural style that emphasizes scalability, simplicity, and statelessness in API design. When developing APIs, RESTful principles provide a framework for creating well-structured, predictable, and scalable services. In this chapter, we will explore the core principles of REST architecture, how to create RESTful endpoints, structure resources and data, version your API, and follow best practices for RESTful API development.

8.1 Principles of REST Architecture

REST architecture is based on six guiding principles that shape the interaction between the client and the server. These principles are designed to improve the performance, scalability, and simplicity of APIs.

1. **Statelessness**
   - In REST, each request from a client to the server must contain all the necessary information for the server to fulfill the request. The server does not retain client state between requests.
   - Every request is independent, and the server does not store the session state. This simplifies the server's logic and improves scalability.
   - Example: When making a request to a resource, the client sends its authentication token and any relevant parameters, instead of relying on

the server to track its session.

2. **Client-Server Separation**

- REST enforces a separation of concerns between the client and the server. The client is responsible for the user interface and presentation, while the server handles data storage and business logic.
- This separation allows both the client and server to evolve independently, improving scalability and maintainability.

3. **Uniform Interface**

- REST APIs should provide a consistent, predictable interface. Resources are identified by URIs (Uniform Resource Identifiers), and interactions with those resources are defined by standard HTTP methods.
- The consistent use of HTTP methods (GET, POST, PUT, DELETE) allows clients to interact with resources in a uniform way.

4. **Cacheability**

- RESTful services can take advantage of caching to improve performance. Responses should define whether they are cacheable and for how long.
- Caching can significantly reduce the number of requests the client sends to the server, improving efficiency.

5. **Layered System**

- REST architecture allows for a layered system in which intermediaries (such as load balancers, proxies, or gateways) can handle specific tasks like security, caching, or logging. The client does not need to know if it's communicating directly with the server or through an intermediary.

6. **Code on Demand (Optional)**

- Servers can extend the functionality of clients by sending executable code (e.g., JavaScript). However, this principle is optional and rarely used in most RESTful API designs.

By following these principles, REST APIs become scalable, flexible, and easy to maintain.

8.2 Creating RESTful Endpoints

In a RESTful API, each resource is accessible through a specific URI, and the standard HTTP methods (GET, POST, PUT, DELETE) define the operations that can be performed on those resources.

1. **Defining Routes and Resources**

A **resource** represents a key entity in your application, such as users, products, or orders. In RESTful design, resources are typically nouns, and each resource is accessed via a URI.

Example:

```
plaintext
Copy code
GET    /api/users      # Retrieve a list of users
GET    /api/users/1    # Retrieve a specific user by ID
POST   /api/users      # Create a new user
PUT    /api/users/1    # Update a user by ID
DELETE /api/users/1    # Delete a user by ID
```

2. **Mapping HTTP Methods to CRUD Operations**

- **GET**: Retrieves data from the server (e.g., fetch a list of resources or a single resource).
- **POST**: Sends data to the server to create a new resource.
- **PUT**: Updates an existing resource or creates a new one if it does not exist.
- **DELETE**: Deletes an existing resource.

Example: Creating RESTful Endpoints in Flask

```python
Copy code
from flask import Flask, jsonify, request

app = Flask(__name__)

# In-memory list of users for demonstration purposes
users = [{'id': 1, 'name': 'John Doe'}, {'id': 2, 'name': 'Jane Doe'}]

@app.route('/api/users', methods=['GET'])
def get_users():
    return jsonify(users)

@app.route('/api/users/<int:user_id>', methods=['GET'])
def get_user(user_id):
    user = next((user for user in users if user['id'] == user_id), None)
    if user:
        return jsonify(user)
    return jsonify({'error': 'User not found'}), 404

@app.route('/api/users', methods=['POST'])
def create_user():
    new_user = request.json
    users.append(new_user)
    return jsonify(new_user), 201

@app.route('/api/users/<int:user_id>'
, methods=['PUT'])
def update_user(user_id):
    user = next((user for user in
 users if user['id'] == user_id), None)
    if user:
        user.update(request.json)
        return jsonify(user)
    return jsonify({'error':
 'User not found'}), 404
```

CHAPTER 8: BUILDING A RESTFUL API WITH FLASK

```python
@app.route('/api/users/<int:user_id>', methods=['DELETE'])
def delete_user(user_id):
    global users
    users = [user for user in users if user['id'] != user_id]
    return jsonify({'message': 'User deleted'}), 204

if __name__ == '__main__':
    app.run(debug=True)
```

In this example:

- /api/users handles both GET requests to retrieve all users and POST requests to create a new user.
- /api/users/<user_id> handles GET, PUT, and DELETE requests to retrieve, update, and delete a user by ID.

8.3 Structuring API Resources and Data

The way you structure resources and data in a RESTful API affects its usability and scalability. Best practices include grouping related resources and organizing URIs in a clear and logical manner.

1. **Nested Resources**

When a resource is a sub-resource of another, use a nested structure in the URL.

Example:

```plaintext
Copy code
GET  /api/users/1/orders    # Get orders for user with ID 1
POST /api/users/1/orders
  # Create a new order for user with ID 1
```

2. **Filtering and Pagination**

For large datasets, you should provide mechanisms to filter, sort, and paginate data to improve performance and client usability.

Example:

```plaintext
Copy code
GET /api/users?page=2&limit=10
    # Pagination
GET /api/users?name=john&sort=created
    # Filtering and sorting
```

3. Relationships Between Resources

If a resource has relationships with other resources (e.g., a user has many orders), you can provide related data in the response or provide links to those resources.

Example:

```json
Copy code
{
  "id": 1,
  "name": "John Doe",
  "orders": [
    {"order_id": 101, "product": "Laptop"},
    {"order_id": 102, "product": "Smartphone"}
  ]
}
```

8.4 Versioning Your API

API versioning ensures backward compatibility, allowing clients to continue using an older version of the API while new features or changes are introduced in newer versions. There are several ways to version your API:

1. URI Versioning

Include the version number in the URL path.

Example:

```plaintext
Copy code
GET /api/v1/users
  # Version 1
GET /api/v2/users
    # Version 2 (newer version with changes)
```

2. Header Versioning

Use a custom header to specify the API version.
Example:

```plaintext
Copy code
GET /api/users
Headers:
  Accept: application/vnd.example.v1+json
```

3. Query Parameter Versioning

Use a query parameter to specify the version.
Example:

```plaintext
Copy code
GET /api/users?version=1
```

4. Best Practices for Versioning

- Start with versioning even if you don't expect major changes soon. It allows you to introduce changes without breaking existing clients.
- Be explicit in the versioning strategy to avoid confusion.
- Avoid making breaking changes to existing versions of the API.

8.5 Best Practices for RESTful API Development

To ensure your REST API is scalable, maintainable, and user-friendly, follow these best practices:

1. Use Consistent Naming Conventions

- Use clear, consistent, and pluralized resource names in the URLs. Avoid verbs in the resource names as the HTTP method already defines the action.
- Example:

```plaintext
Copy code
/api/users (GET)      # Retrieves users
/api/users/1 (GET)
# Retrieves user with ID 1
```

2. Use Appropriate HTTP Methods

- Always use the correct HTTP method for the appropriate action (e.g., GET for retrieving data, POST for creating new data, PUT for updating existing data, and DELETE for removing data).

3. Return Proper Status Codes

- Return the appropriate HTTP status codes to indicate the outcome of the request. Common status codes include:
- 200 OK: The request was successful.
- 201 Created: A new resource was created.
- 400 Bad Request: The request was malformed or invalid.
- 404 Not Found: The requested resource could not be found.
- 500 Internal Server Error: A server error occurred.

Chapter 9: Testing and Debugging Flask APIs

Testing and debugging are critical components of the software development lifecycle, especially for APIs that must perform reliably and return expected results. This chapter covers the fundamentals of API testing, including how to write unit tests for Flask APIs, use tools like Postman and Curl for manual testing, debug Flask applications effectively, and handle edge cases and failures gracefully.

9.1 Introduction to API Testing

API testing is the process of verifying that an API meets its expected functionality, performance, and security requirements. This involves checking whether the API returns the correct responses for given inputs, handles errors appropriately, and performs under load.

Importance of API Testing:
- **Functionality Verification**: Ensures that the API behaves as expected and meets the specified requirements.
- **Performance Testing**: Evaluates how the API performs under various conditions, including high load and concurrency.
- **Security Testing**: Checks for vulnerabilities that could be exploited by malicious actors.
- **Integration Testing**: Verifies that the API integrates correctly with other

services and components.

API testing can be conducted manually or automated. Automated tests are particularly valuable in continuous integration and delivery (CI/CD) environments, where code changes need to be validated quickly and frequently.

9.2 Writing Unit Tests for Flask APIs

Unit tests are a form of automated testing that focuses on testing individual components or functions of the application in isolation. Flask provides a testing framework to facilitate unit testing of your application.

Step 1: Setting Up a Test Configuration

Create a test configuration for your Flask app. This can be done in a new file named test_config.py or directly in your test suite. A common practice is to use a separate testing database.

Example test_config.py:

```python
Copy code
class TestConfig:
    TESTING = True
    SQLALCHEMY_DATABASE_URI =
 'sqlite:///:memory:'
# In-memory database for testing
    SQLALCHEMY_TRACK_MODIFICATIONS = False
```

Step 2: Writing Unit Tests

Flask's built-in unittest framework can be used to write unit tests. Create a new file, test_app.py, and define your test cases.

Example:

```python
Copy code
import unittest
from app import create_app, db

class BasicAPITestCase(unittest.TestCase):
```

CHAPTER 9: TESTING AND DEBUGGING FLASK APIS

```python
    def setUp(self):
        """Set up the test environment and create the app."""
        self.app = create_app(TestConfig)
        self.client = self.app.test_client()  # Create a test client
        with self.app.app_context():
            db.create_all()  # Create the database

    def tearDown(self):
        """Clean up after each test."""
        with self.app.app_context():
            db.drop_all()  # Drop the database

    def test_get_users(self):
        """Test the GET /api/users endpoint."""
        response = self.client.get('/api/users')
        self.assertEqual(response.status_code, 200)
        self.assertIsInstance(response.json, list)  # Check that response is a list

    def test_create_user(self):
        """Test the POST /api/users endpoint."""
        response = self.client.post('/api/users',
            json={'username': 'testuser', 'email': 'test@example.com'})
        self.assertEqual(response.status_code, 201)
        self.assertIn('testuser', response.json['message'])

if __name__ == '__main__':
    unittest.main()
```

In this example:

- **setUp()**: Configures the test environment by creating a new app instance and a test client. It also creates the database schema.

- **tearDown()**: Cleans up after each test by dropping the database.
- **Unit Tests**: Two simple tests verify that the GET /api/users and POST /api/users endpoints behave as expected.

Step 3: Running Tests

You can run your tests from the command line:

```bash
Copy code
python -m unittest test_app.py
```

This command executes all tests in the specified file, and you will see the results in the terminal.

9.3 Testing API Endpoints with Postman and Curl

While unit tests are crucial for automated testing, manual testing tools like Postman and Curl provide a way to interactively test API endpoints. These tools are valuable for quick checks during development and debugging.

Using Postman

Postman is a powerful API client that allows you to send requests and view responses easily. You can create collections of API endpoints, organize them, and even automate testing.

Getting Started with Postman:

1. **Download and Install**: Visit the Postman website to download and install the application.
2. **Creating a Request**:

- Open Postman and create a new request.
- Select the HTTP method (GET, POST, etc.).
- Enter the URL of the API endpoint you want to test.
- For POST or PUT requests, you can enter the request body in JSON format.

1. **Send the Request**: Click the "Send" button to send the request and view the response.

Example of Testing a POST Request:

- Create a new user by sending a POST request to http://127.0.0.1:5000/api/users with a JSON body:

```json
Copy code
{
  "username": "testuser",
  "email": "test@example.com"
}
```

Postman will display the response, including the status code and any returned data.

Using Curl

Curl is a command-line tool for transferring data using various protocols. It is lightweight and often used for testing APIs in scripts.

Basic Curl Commands:

- **GET Request**:

```bash
Copy code
curl -X GET http://127.0.0.1:5000/api/users
```

- **POST Request**:

```bash
Copy code
curl -X POST -H "Content-Type:
 application/json" -d '{"username":"testuser",
"email":"test@example.com"}' http://127.0.0.1:5000/api/users
```

- **Including Headers**: You can include authentication tokens or other headers as needed:

```bash
Copy code
curl -H "Authorization: Bearer your_token"
http://127.0.0.1:5000/api/protected
```

Curl is particularly useful for quickly testing endpoints without needing a graphical interface.

9.4 Debugging Flask Applications

Debugging is a critical part of development, allowing you to identify and resolve issues quickly. Flask provides several tools and techniques to help with debugging.

1. **Using Flask Debug Mode**

Flask has a built-in debug mode that provides detailed error messages and a debugger console in the browser.

To enable debug mode, set debug=True when running the application:

```python
Copy code
if __name__ == '__main__':
    app.run(debug=True)
```

When an error occurs, Flask displays a detailed error traceback in the browser, showing the line of code that caused the error and the context of the application at that moment.

2. Using Debugger and Breakpoints

You can insert breakpoints in your code using the Python debugger (pdb). This allows you to pause execution and inspect variables at specific points in your application.

Example:

```python
Copy code
import pdb

@app.route('/api/debug')
def debug_example():
    pdb.set_trace()  # Execution will pause here
    return jsonify({'message': 'This will be inspected'})
```

When the endpoint is accessed, the application will pause execution, allowing you to examine variables and step through the code interactively.

3. Logging

As mentioned in the previous chapter, using logging is essential for tracking down issues in production. Set up logging to capture important events, warnings, and errors.

Example:

```python
Copy code
import logging

logging.basicConfig(level=logging.DEBUG)

@app.route('/api/logging_example')
def logging_example():
    app.logger.debug('This is a debug message')
    return jsonify({'message': 'Check your logs'})
```

Debugging logs can provide insight into the application's behavior and help identify problems.

9.5 Handling Edge Cases and Failures in APIs

APIs must be robust and capable of handling unexpected input or conditions gracefully. Proper error handling ensures that clients receive meaningful error messages and can recover from issues.

1. Input Validation

Validate all incoming data to ensure it meets expected formats and constraints. Use appropriate HTTP status codes to signal validation errors.

Example:

```python
Copy code
@app.route('/api/users', methods=['POST'])
def create_user():
    data = request.json
    if 'username' not in data or 'email' not in data:
        return jsonify({'error': 'Username and email are required'}), 400
    # Proceed with user creation...
```

2. Graceful Error Handling

Instead of returning generic error messages, provide clear and actionable feedback to the client.

Example:

```python
Copy code
@app.errorhandler(500)
def internal_server_error(error):
    app.logger.error(f'Server Error: {error}')
    return jsonify({'error': 'An unexpected error occurred. Please try again later.'}), 500
```

3. Testing for Edge Cases

Consider edge cases that may arise in your application, such as:

- Handling large payloads.
- Dealing with timeouts or slow responses from external services.
- Ensuring the API behaves as expected when receiving malformed requests.

Write tests that specifically address these edge cases to ensure that your API can handle them gracefully.

Chapter 10: Flask Extensions for API Development

Flask's lightweight and modular architecture allows developers to extend its capabilities easily through a variety of extensions. These extensions add useful functionality and simplify common tasks associated with API development. In this chapter, we will explore several popular Flask extensions, including Flask-RESTful, Flask-Swagger, Flask-JWT-Extended, Flask-CORS, and Flask-Limiter.

10.1 Flask-RESTful: Simplifying API Development

Flask-RESTful is an extension that simplifies the creation of RESTful APIs in Flask. It provides tools to create resource-oriented APIs by abstracting some of the complexity associated with routing and response handling.

Key Features of Flask-RESTful

- **Resource-Based Routing**: Defines resources and handles the mapping of HTTP methods to resource methods (GET, POST, PUT, DELETE).
- **Automatic Request Parsing**: Automatically parses incoming request data (JSON, form data) and handles common content types.
- **Built-In Support for Error Handling**: Simplifies error handling by providing a consistent way to respond with error messages.

Example: Using Flask-RESTful

Step 1: Install Flask-RESTful:

```bash
Copy code
pip install Flask-RESTful
```

Step 2: Define Resources Using Flask-RESTful:

```python
Copy code
from flask import Flask
from flask_restful import Resource, Api

app = Flask(__name__)
api = Api(app)

# Mock user data
users = [{'id': 1, 'name': 'John Doe'},
{'id': 2, 'name': 'Jane Doe'}]

class User(Resource):
    def get(self, user_id):
        user = next
((user for user in users if user['id']
 == user_id), None)
        if user:
            return user, 200
        return {'error': 'User not found'}, 404

    def post(self):
        # Handle user creation logic here...
        pass

api.add_resource(User,
 '/api/users/<int:user_id>')
 # Define the endpoint

if __name__ == '__main__':
```

```
app.run(debug=True)
```

In this example:

- We create a resource class (User) that defines methods to handle GET requests for user data.
- The add_resource method maps the resource to a specific URI, allowing Flask-RESTful to handle the routing automatically.

10.2 Flask-Swagger: Auto-Documenting Your API

Flask-Swagger is an extension that enables automatic generation of API documentation using the OpenAPI specification (formerly known as Swagger). This documentation is invaluable for both developers and consumers of the API.

Key Features of Flask-Swagger

- **Auto-Generated Documentation**: Generates interactive API documentation that can be accessed via a web interface.
- **Ease of Use**: Provides decorators to annotate your API endpoints and automatically create the OpenAPI documentation.

Example: Using Flask-Swagger

Step 1: Install Flask-Swagger:

```
bash
Copy code
pip install flask-swagger-ui
```

Step 2: Integrate Flask-Swagger into Your Application:

```
python
Copy code
```

CHAPTER 10: FLASK EXTENSIONS FOR API DEVELOPMENT

```python
from flask import Flask
from flask_restful import Api
from flask_swagger_ui import get_swaggerui_blueprint

app = Flask(__name__)
api = Api(app)

# Swagger UI configuration
SWAGGER_URL = '/swagger'
API_URL = '/static/swagger.json'
 # URL for the Swagger API documentation

swaggerui_blueprint = get_swaggerui_blueprint(
    SWAGGER_URL,
    API_URL,
    config={
        'app_name': "Flask API"
    }
)

app.register_blueprint(swaggerui_blueprint, url_prefix=SWAGGER_URL)

@app.route('/api/users')
def get_users():
    """Returns a list of users."""
    return [{'id': 1, 'name': 'John Doe'},
{'id': 2, 'name': 'Jane Doe'}]

if __name__ == '__main__':
    app.run(debug=True)
```

In this example:

- We configure Flask-Swagger to serve the documentation at /swagger.
- The Swagger UI provides an interactive interface for exploring the API, making it easy to test endpoints and view documentation.

Creating a Swagger JSON File

To generate the Swagger documentation, create a JSON file that describes your API. This file should include details about endpoints, request/response structures, and any parameters used.

Example swagger.json:

```json
Copy code
{
  "swagger": "2.0",
  "info": {
    "description": "This is a sample API",
    "version": "1.0.0",
    "title": "Flask API"
  },
  "paths": {
    "/api/users": {
      "get": {
        "summary": "Get all users",
        "responses": {
          "200": {
            "description": "A list of users",
            "schema": {
              "type": "array",
              "items": {
                "type": "object",
                "properties": {
                  "id": {
                    "type": "integer"
                  },
                  "name": {
                    "type": "string"
                  }
                }
              }
            }
          }
        }
      }
    }
  }
}
```

}

You can host this file at the specified API_URL to allow Swagger UI to fetch it.

10.3 Flask-JWT-Extended: Advanced JWT Authentication

Flask-JWT-Extended is an extension that simplifies the implementation of JWT-based authentication in Flask applications. It offers features such as token refreshing, blacklisting, and more.

Key Features of Flask-JWT-Extended

- **Token Creation and Verification**: Easily create and verify JWTs with a few decorators.
- **Token Refreshing**: Support for refreshing access tokens.
- **Blacklisting Tokens**: Ability to revoke tokens when needed.

Example: Using Flask-JWT-Extended

Step 1: Install Flask-JWT-Extended:

```bash
Copy code
pip install Flask-JWT-Extended
```

Step 2: Implement JWT Authentication:

```python
Copy code
from flask import Flask, jsonify, request
from flask_jwt_extended import JWTManager, create_access_token, jwt_required

app = Flask(__name__)
app.config['JWT_SECRET_KEY'] = 'your_jwt_secret_key'  # Change this in production
jwt = JWTManager(app)
```

```python
@app.route('/api/login', methods=['POST'])
def login():
    username = request.json.get('username')
    password = request.json.get('password')

    # Here you should validate the username and password
    if username == 'john' and password == 'hello123':
        access_token = create_access_token(identity=username)
        return jsonify(access_token=access_token)

    return jsonify({'error': 'Invalid credentials'}), 401

@app.route('/api/protected', methods=['GET'])
@jwt_required()
def protected():
    current_user = get_jwt_identity()
    return jsonify({'message': f'Hello, {current_user}! This is protected data.'})

if __name__ == '__main__':
    app.run(debug=True)
```

In this example:

- The /api/login route validates user credentials and returns a JWT upon successful login.
- The /api/protected route requires a valid JWT to access the protected resource.

10.4 Flask-CORS: Enabling Cross-Origin Resource Sharing

Flask-CORS is an extension that allows you to enable Cross-Origin Resource Sharing (CORS) for your Flask application. CORS is essential when your API is accessed from a different origin (domain, protocol, or port) than the server hosting the API.

Key Features of Flask-CORS

- **Flexible Configuration**: Allows you to customize CORS behavior for specific routes or for the entire application.
- **Supports Preflight Requests**: Automatically handles CORS preflight requests for HTTP methods that require it.

Example: Using Flask-CORS

Step 1: Install Flask-CORS:

```bash
Copy code
pip install Flask-CORS
```

Step 2: Enable CORS in Your Application:

```python
Copy code
from flask import Flask
from flask_cors import CORS

app = Flask(__name__)
CORS(app)  # Enable CORS for all routes

@app.route('/api/data', methods=['GET'])
def get_data():
    return {'data': 'This is some data'}

if __name__ == '__main__':
    app.run(debug=True)
```

In this example, CORS is enabled for all routes by simply passing the app instance to CORS(). You can also customize it to apply only to specific routes or origins.

Customizing CORS

You can customize CORS behavior by specifying allowed origins, methods, and headers:

```python
Copy code
CORS(app, resources={r"/api/*": {"origins": "http://example.com"}})
```

In this case, only requests from http://example.com are allowed to access the /api/* endpoints.

10.5 Flask-Limiter: Rate Limiting API Endpoints

Flask-Limiter is an extension that provides rate limiting functionality to your Flask application. Rate limiting is essential for protecting APIs from abuse and ensuring fair usage among clients.

Key Features of Flask-Limiter

- **Flexible Rate Limiting**: Allows you to define limits per route, client IP, or any other criteria.
- **Custom Response on Rate Limit Exceeded**: You can customize the response returned when the rate limit is exceeded.

Example: Using Flask-Limiter

Step 1: Install Flask-Limiter:

```bash
Copy code
pip install Flask-Limiter
```

Step 2: Implement Rate Limiting:

```python
Copy code
```

CHAPTER 10: FLASK EXTENSIONS FOR API DEVELOPMENT

```
from flask import Flask, jsonify
```

Chapter 11: Deploying Flask APIs

Deploying a Flask API is a crucial step in the development lifecycle, allowing your application to be accessed by users or clients. Proper deployment ensures that the API runs efficiently, securely, and reliably. In this chapter, we will discuss how to prepare your Flask API for production, deploy it on popular platforms like Heroku, AWS, and Google Cloud, use Docker for deployment, and configure Gunicorn and Nginx as the web server and reverse proxy for Flask applications.

11.1 Preparing Your Flask API for Production

Before deploying your Flask API, it's essential to prepare the application for production to ensure performance, security, and reliability.

Key Steps in Preparation

1. **Configuration Management**:

- Use environment variables to manage configuration settings for different environments (development, testing, production).
- Flask provides a config object where you can define settings based on the environment.

1. Example:

```python
Copy code
import os

class Config:
    SECRET_KEY = os.environ.get('SECRET_KEY') or
    'your_default_secret_key'
    DEBUG = False
    SQLALCHEMY_DATABASE_URI = os.environ.get('DATABASE_URL')
```

1. **Error Handling**:

- Implement robust error handling and logging to capture errors and provide useful feedback.
- Use custom error handlers to return structured JSON responses for API consumers.

1. **Use a Production WSGI Server**:

- Flask's built-in server is not suitable for production. Instead, use a WSGI server like Gunicorn or uWSGI to serve your application.

1. **Testing**:

- Ensure your application is thoroughly tested, including unit tests, integration tests, and end-to-end tests.

1. **Performance Optimization**:

- Consider performance optimizations such as caching, database indexing, and optimizing resource-heavy operations.

1. **Security Measures**:

- Implement security measures such as HTTPS, input validation, and using secure authentication methods (e.g., JWT).
- Regularly update dependencies to mitigate vulnerabilities.

11.2 Deploying Flask Apps on Heroku

Heroku is a cloud platform that enables developers to build, run, and operate applications entirely in the cloud. It is a popular choice for deploying Flask applications due to its simplicity and ease of use.

Step-by-Step Deployment on Heroku

1. **Create a Heroku Account**:

- Sign up for a free Heroku account if you don't have one.

1. **Install the Heroku CLI**:

- Install the Heroku Command Line Interface (CLI) on your machine.

1. **Prepare Your Application**:

- Ensure your Flask app is set up for deployment with the necessary files:
- **Procfile**: A file that tells Heroku how to run your application.
- Example Procfile:

```plaintext
Copy code
web: gunicorn app:app
```

- **requirements.txt**: A file that lists all dependencies for your application. You can create it using:

```bash
Copy code
pip freeze > requirements.txt
```

1. **Initialize a Git Repository**:

- If your application is not already in a Git repository, initialize one:

```bash
Copy code
git init
git add .
git commit -m "Initial commit"
```

1. **Create a New Heroku App**:

- Use the Heroku CLI to create a new app:

```bash
Copy code
heroku create your-app-name
```

1. **Deploy Your Application**:

- Push your code to Heroku:

```bash
Copy code
git push heroku master
```

1. **Open Your Application**:

- After deployment, you can open your application in the browser:

```bash
Copy code
heroku open
```

1. **Manage Environment Variables**:

- Set environment variables using the Heroku CLI:

```bash
Copy code
heroku config:set SECRET
_KEY=your_secret_key
```

Heroku takes care of the underlying infrastructure, allowing you to focus on building your application.

11.3 Deploying Flask APIs on AWS and Google Cloud

Both **AWS (Amazon Web Services)** and **Google Cloud Platform (GCP)** offer robust solutions for deploying Flask applications. They provide flexibility, scalability, and various services to suit different needs.

Deploying on AWS

1. **Use Elastic Beanstalk**:

- AWS Elastic Beanstalk is an easy-to-use service for deploying and scaling web applications.
- Prepare a Dockerrun.aws.json or use the standard Elastic Beanstalk setup.

1. **Set Up an EC2 Instance**:

- Alternatively, you can set up an EC2 instance to host your Flask app. Install required packages (like Python, Flask, and Gunicorn) on the instance and use a web server like Nginx as a reverse proxy.

1. **Use AWS RDS**:

- For database needs, consider using Amazon RDS (Relational Database Service) for managed database solutions.

Deploying on Google Cloud

1. **Use Google App Engine**:

- Google App Engine allows you to build and host applications in the cloud. Create an app.yaml file to configure your app.

1. Example app.yaml:

```yaml
Copy code
runtime: python39
entrypoint: gunicorn -b :$PORT app:app

handlers:
- url: /.*
  script: auto
```

1. **Use Google Compute Engine**:

- Set up a virtual machine on Google Compute Engine and configure it to run your Flask app, similar to how you would on AWS EC2.

1. **Use Google Cloud SQL**:

- For database services, Google Cloud SQL offers managed databases that can be easily integrated with your Flask application.

11.4 Using Docker for Flask API Deployment

Docker is a platform that enables developers to automate the deployment of applications inside lightweight containers. Docker containers are portable and can run consistently across various environments.

Step-by-Step Deployment with Docker

1. **Create a Dockerfile**:

- Create a Dockerfile in your Flask application directory that defines how to build the Docker image.

1. **Example Dockerfile**:

```dockerfile
Copy code
FROM python:3.9

WORKDIR /app

COPY requirements.txt requirements.txt
RUN pip install -r requirements.txt

COPY . .
```

```
CMD ["gunicorn", "-b",
 "0.0.0.0:5000", "app:app"]
```

1. **Build the Docker Image**:

- Build the Docker image using the following command:

```bash
Copy code
docker build -t your_flask_app .
```

1. **Run the Docker Container**:

- Run the container using:

```bash
Copy code
docker run -p 5000:5000 your_flask_app
```

1. This command maps port 5000 of the container to port 5000 of your host machine.
2. **Deploy to a Cloud Provider**:

- You can deploy your Dockerized Flask app to cloud providers that support Docker, such as AWS ECS, Google Kubernetes Engine, or Heroku.

11.5 Configuring Gunicorn and Nginx for Flask APIs

For production deployment, using a WSGI server like **Gunicorn** in combination with a reverse proxy like **Nginx** enhances performance and security.

1. **Installing Gunicorn**:

- Install Gunicorn in your Flask app environment:

```bash
Copy code
pip install gunicorn
```

2. **Running Gunicorn**:

- Use Gunicorn to serve your Flask app:

```bash
Copy code
gunicorn -w 4 -b 0.0.0.0:5000 app:app
```

Here, -w 4 specifies the number of worker processes to handle requests.

3. **Setting Up Nginx**:

- Install Nginx on your server (e.g., using apt for Ubuntu):

```bash
Copy code
sudo apt install nginx
```

- Configure Nginx to act as a reverse proxy. Create a new configuration

CHAPTER 11: DEPLOYING FLASK APIS

file in /etc/nginx/sites-available/your_flask_app:

Example Nginx configuration:

```nginx
Copy code
server {
    listen 80;
    server_name your_domain.com;
 # Replace with your domain or IP address

    location / {
        proxy_pass http://127.0.0.1:5000;
  # Forward requests to Gunicorn
        proxy_set_header Host $host;
        proxy_set_header X-Real-IP $remote_addr;
        proxy_set_header X-Forwarded-For $proxy_add_x_forwarded_for;
        proxy_set_header X-Forwarded-Proto $scheme;
    }
}
```

- Enable the configuration by creating a symlink to sites-enabled:

```bash
Copy code
sudo ln -s /etc/nginx/sites-available/your_flask_app /etc/nginx/sites-enabled
```

- Test the Nginx configuration:

```bash
Copy code
sudo nginx -t
```

- Restart Nginx to apply changes:

```bash
Copy code
sudo systemctl restart nginx
```

4. **Security Measures**:

- Consider securing your application with HTTPS using **Let's Encrypt** for free SSL certificates.

Chapter 12: API Rate Limiting and Caching in Flask

Rate limiting and caching are essential strategies for improving the performance, reliability, and security of APIs. Rate limiting protects your API from abuse and ensures fair usage among clients, while caching enhances response times and reduces server load. In this chapter, we will explore the concepts of rate limiting and caching, how to implement them in Flask using appropriate extensions, and how to configure cache expiry and invalidations.

12.1 Introduction to Rate Limiting for APIs

Rate Limiting is a technique used to control the number of requests a client can make to an API within a specified time frame. This practice is crucial for preventing abuse, managing server load, and ensuring fair access for all users.

Why Implement Rate Limiting?

- **Prevent Abuse**: Protects your API from malicious users who may try to overwhelm your server with excessive requests.
- **Resource Management**: Helps manage server resources by limiting the number of concurrent requests.
- **Enhanced User Experience**: Ensures that all users have fair access to API resources and can expect consistent performance.

Common Rate Limiting Strategies

- **Fixed Window**: Limits the number of requests allowed in a fixed time window (e.g., 100 requests per minute).
- **Sliding Window**: Similar to fixed window but allows for a smoother flow of requests by tracking the time of individual requests.
- **Leaky Bucket**: Processes requests at a constant rate and queues excess requests, allowing for burst capacity while managing long-term rate limits.

12.2 Implementing Rate Limiting with Flask-Limiter

Flask-Limiter is an extension for Flask that provides rate limiting functionality. It allows developers to apply rate limits on routes, based on various criteria such as IP address or user authentication.

Step-by-Step Implementation

Step 1: Install Flask-Limiter:

```bash
Copy code
pip install Flask-Limiter
```

Step 2: Configure Flask-Limiter:

```python
Copy code
from flask import Flask, jsonify
from flask_limiter import Limiter
from flask_limiter.util import import
get_remote_address

app = Flask(__name__)
limiter = Limiter(
    key_func=get_remote_address,
 # Limit based on client IP
```

```
    default_limits=["100 per minute"]
# Default limit for all routes
)

@app.route('/api/resource')
@limiter.limit("10 per minute")
# Specific limit for this route
def get_resource():
    return jsonify({'message':
'This is a rate-limited resource.'})


if __name__ == '__main__':
    app.run(debug=True)
```

In this example:

- **Limiter**: An instance of Limiter is created, specifying that limits should be based on the remote IP address.
- **default_limits**: Sets a default limit of 100 requests per minute for all routes.
- **Route-specific Limit**: The @limiter.limit("10 per minute") decorator applies a specific limit for the /api/resource endpoint.

3. **Custom Rate Limit Responses**

You can customize the response returned when a client exceeds the rate limit by using the @limiter.error_handler decorator.

Example:

```
python
Copy code
@limiter.error_handler
def ratelimit_error(e):
    return jsonify
(error="ratelimit exceeded",
```

```
message=str(e.description)), 429
```

This response provides a structured JSON message when a user exceeds their rate limit.

12.3 Using Flask-Caching for Optimizing API Performance

Flask-Caching is an extension that adds caching capabilities to Flask applications, allowing you to store the results of expensive operations, such as database queries or API responses. Caching improves performance and reduces load on your server.

Key Features of Flask-Caching

- **Multiple Backends**: Supports various caching backends such as Redis, Memcached, and simple in-memory caching.
- **Cache Control**: Provides mechanisms to control cache expiry and invalidation.

Step-by-Step Implementation

Step 1: Install Flask-Caching:

```bash
Copy code
pip install Flask-Caching
```

Step 2: Configure Flask-Caching:

```python
Copy code
from flask import Flask, jsonify
from flask_caching import Cache

app = Flask(__name__)
cache = Cache(app, config=
{'CACHE_TYPE': 'simple'})
  # Using simple in-memory caching
```

CHAPTER 12: API RATE LIMITING AND CACHING IN FLASK

```
@app.route('/api/data')
@cache.cached(timeout=60)
# Cache the response for 60 seconds
def get_data():
    # Simulate an expensive operation
    return jsonify
({'data': 'This data is cached!'})

if __name__ == '__main__':
    app.run(debug=True)
```

In this example:

- **Cache**: An instance of Cache is created with a simple in-memory configuration.
- **Caching Responses**: The @cache.cached(timeout=60) decorator caches the response for 60 seconds, meaning subsequent requests within that timeframe will receive the cached response instead of re-executing the function.

12.4 Configuring Cache Expiry and Invalidations

Managing cache expiry and invalidations is essential to ensure that clients receive up-to-date information and to avoid serving stale data.

1. **Setting Cache Expiry**

When using Flask-Caching, you can set an expiry time for cached responses using the timeout parameter in the @cache.cached() decorator.

Example:

```python
Copy code
@cache.cached(timeout=300)
  # Cache the response for 5 minutes
```

2. **Invalidating Cache**

You may need to manually invalidate or remove cached data, especially when the underlying data changes.

- **Clear Specific Cache**: Use the cache.delete() method to clear a specific cached view.

Example:

```python
Copy code
@app.route('/api/clear_cache')
def clear_cache():
    cache.delete('get_data')
# Clear cache for a specific view
    return jsonify({'message': 'Cache cleared!'})
```

- **Clear All Cache**: Use cache.clear() to remove all cached data.

Example:

```python
Copy code
@app.route('/api/clear_all_cache')
def clear_all_cache():
    cache.clear()  # Clear all cached data
    return jsonify({'message': 'All cache cleared!'})
```

3. Configuring Cache Control Headers

To ensure that clients know when cached data will expire, you can set appropriate cache control headers in the response.

Example:

CHAPTER 12: API RATE LIMITING AND CACHING IN FLASK

```python
Copy code
from flask import make_response

@app.route('/api/data_with_headers')
@cache.cached(timeout=60)
def data_with_headers():
    response = make_response
(jsonify({'data':
'This data has cache control!'}))
    response.headers['Cache-Control'] =
'public, max-age=60'
 # Set cache control headers
    return response
```

Chapter 13: Handling File Uploads and Downloads

Handling file uploads and downloads is a common requirement in many web applications, including APIs. Flask provides several tools to manage file transfers securely and efficiently. In this chapter, we will explore how to create file upload endpoints, validate and secure uploaded files, serve static files, and handle file downloads in Flask.

13.1 File Upload API Endpoints in Flask

Creating an API endpoint for file uploads allows clients to send files to the server. Flask simplifies this process by providing utilities for handling file data in requests.

Step-by-Step Implementation of File Uploads

Step 1: Setting Up the Flask App

First, ensure you have Flask installed and create a simple Flask application.

```
bash
Copy code
pip install Flask
```

Step 2: Creating a File Upload Endpoint

Here's an example of how to create an endpoint to handle file uploads:

CHAPTER 13: HANDLING FILE UPLOADS AND DOWNLOADS

```python
Copy code
from flask import Flask, request, jsonify

app = Flask(__name__)

# Configure the upload folder
UPLOAD_FOLDER = 'uploads'
# Ensure this directory exists
app.config['UPLOAD_FOLDER'] = UPLOAD_FOLDER

@app.route('/api/upload', methods=['POST'])
def upload_file():
    if 'file' not in request.files:
        return jsonify({'error':
 'No file part'}), 400

    file = request.files['file']

    if file.filename == '':
        return jsonify({'error':
 'No selected file'}), 400

    # Save the file
    file.save(f"
{app.config['UPLOAD_FOLDER']}/
{file.filename}")
    return jsonify({'message': 'File uploaded successfully'}), 201

if __name__ == '__main__':
    app.run(debug=True)
```

In this example:

- The /api/upload endpoint handles POST requests to upload files.
- The request.files attribute is used to access the uploaded file.
- The uploaded file is saved to the specified directory.

Testing the File Upload Endpoint

You can test the file upload functionality using tools like Postman or Curl. Example using Curl:

```bash
Copy code
curl -X POST -F "file=@path_to_your_file" http://127.0.0.1:5000/api/upload
```

Make sure to replace path_to_your_file with the actual file path you want to upload.

13.2 Validating and Securing File Uploads

When allowing file uploads, it's crucial to validate and secure the files to prevent various attacks, such as file injection or overwriting existing files.

Key Security Measures

1. **File Type Validation**:

- Only allow specific file types based on your application requirements. You can use the filename property of the uploaded file to validate the extension.

Example:

```python
Copy code
ALLOWED_EXTENSIONS = {'txt', 'pdf', 'png', 'jpg', 'jpeg', 'gif'}

def allowed_file(filename):
    return '.' in filename and filename.rsplit('.', 1)[1].lower() in ALLOWED_EXTENSIONS
```

Modify the upload function to check if the file type is allowed:

CHAPTER 13: HANDLING FILE UPLOADS AND DOWNLOADS

```python
Copy code
if not allowed_file(file.filename):
    return jsonify({'error':
'File type not allowed'}), 400
```

1. **File Size Limitations**:

- Limit the size of the files that can be uploaded to prevent denial-of-service attacks. You can set a maximum file size in your Flask app configuration.

Example:

```python
Copy code
app.config['MAX_CONTENT_LENGTH']
= 16 * 1024 * 1024    # Limit to 16 MB
```

1. **File Name Sanitization**:

- Sanitize file names to avoid issues with special characters or path traversal vulnerabilities. Use a secure method to generate a safe file name.

Example:

```python
Copy code
import secure_filename

filename = secure_filename(file.filename)
file.save(f"{app.config[
'UPLOAD_FOLDER']}/{filename}")
```

13.3 Serving Static Files with Flask

Flask can serve static files directly from a specified directory, allowing clients to access resources like images, documents, and downloadable files.

Step-by-Step Configuration for Static File Serving

1. **Set the Static Folder**:

- By default, Flask serves static files from the static folder in your project. You can specify a different directory if needed.

Example:

```python
Copy code
app = Flask(__name__, static_folder='uploads')
# Serve from uploads directory
```

1. **Accessing Static Files**:

- Files in the static folder can be accessed using the URL /static/<filename>.

Example:

```python
Copy code
@app.route('/uploads/<path:filename>')
def uploaded_file(filename):
    return send_from_directory
(app.config['UPLOAD_FOLDER'], filename)
```

1. **Using send_from_directory**:

- The send_from_directory() function serves files securely from a specified directory.

Example:

```python
Copy code
from flask import send_from_directory

@app.route('/files/<filename>')
def serve_file(filename):
    return send_from_directory(app.config['UPLOAD_FOLDER'], filename)
```

Testing Static File Serving

You can test static file serving by accessing a file directly in the browser or using Curl:

```bash
Copy code
curl http://127.0.0.1:5000/files/your_uploaded_file.txt
```

13.4 Handling File Downloads with Flask APIs

In addition to uploading files, you may want to implement endpoints that allow clients to download files stored on the server.

Step-by-Step Implementation of File Downloads

1. **Creating a File Download Endpoint**:

Using the send_from_directory() function makes it easy to implement file downloads.

Example:

```python
from flask import Flask, send_from_directory

app = Flask(__name__)
UPLOAD_FOLDER = 'uploads'
app.config['UPLOAD_FOLDER'] = UPLOAD_FOLDER

@app.route('/api/download/<filename>',
 methods=['GET'])
def download_file(filename):
    return send_from_directory
(app.config['UPLOAD_FOLDER'], filename, as_attachment=True)

if __name__ == '__main__':
    app.run(debug=True)
```

In this example:

- The /api/download/<filename> endpoint allows users to download a specified file from the uploads directory.
- The as_attachment=True parameter prompts the browser to download the file rather than display it.

1. **Testing the Download Endpoint**:

You can test the file download functionality using Curl or a web browser. Example using Curl:

```bash
curl -O http://127.0.0.1:5000/api/
download/your_uploaded_file.txt
```

The -O flag saves the file with the same name as it has on the server.

Chapter 14: Advanced Flask API Features

Flask is a versatile framework that supports various advanced features to enhance your API's capabilities. In this chapter, we will explore real-time communication with Flask-SocketIO, implement pagination in API responses, create webhooks, manage API throttling and resource limiting, and build GraphQL APIs using Flask.

14.1 Real-Time APIs with Flask-SocketIO

Flask-SocketIO is an extension that enables real-time communication between clients and servers using WebSockets. This capability allows your API to push updates to clients instantly, making it ideal for applications that require real-time features like chat applications, notifications, or live data feeds.

Step-by-Step Implementation of Flask-SocketIO

Step 1: Install Flask-SocketIO:

```
bash
Copy code
pip install flask-socketio
```

Step 2: Setting Up Flask-SocketIO:

```python
Copy code
from flask import Flask, render_template
from flask_socketio import SocketIO

app = Flask(__name__)
socketio = SocketIO(app)

@app.route('/')
def index():
    return render_template('index.html')
 # Serve a simple HTML page

@socketio.on('message')
def handle_message(msg):
    print(f"Received message: {msg}")
    socketio.send(msg)   #
 Echo the received message back to the client

if __name__ == '__main__':
    socketio.run(app)
```

In this example:

- We create a basic Flask application and initialize SocketIO.
- The @socketio.on('message') decorator listens for incoming messages from clients and echoes them back.

Step 3: Creating a Simple Client (index.html):

```html
Copy code
<!DOCTYPE html>
<html lang="en">
<head>
    <meta charset="UTF-8">
    <title>Flask-SocketIO Example</title>
```

CHAPTER 14: ADVANCED FLASK API FEATURES

```html
    <script src="https://cdnjs.cloudflare.
com/ajax/libs/socket.
io/4.0.1/socket.io.js"></script>
</head>
<body>
    <h1>Flask-SocketIO Example</h1>
    <input id="message" placeholder="Enter message">
    <button onclick="sendMessage()">Send</button>

    <script>
        const socket = io();

        socket.on('message', function(msg) {
            alert('Message received: ' + msg);
        });

        function sendMessage() {
            const messageInput =
            document.getElementById('message');
            const message = messageInput.value;
            socket.send(message);
            messageInput.value = '';
  // Clear the input field
        }
    </script>
</body>
</html>
```

In this HTML file:

- We include the Socket.IO client library and set up a simple interface for sending messages to the server.
- The client connects to the server and listens for messages, displaying them in an alert.

Testing Real-Time Communication

1. Run your Flask app.

2. Open multiple browser tabs pointing to the app.
3. Send messages from one tab and observe the responses in all connected clients.

14.2 Pagination in API Responses

Pagination is a technique used to break down large datasets into manageable chunks. This is crucial for improving API performance and user experience especially when returning lists of resources.

Step-by-Step Implementation of Pagination

1. **Define the Pagination Logic**:

You can implement pagination by accepting query parameters for page and per_page (number of items per page).

Example:

```python
Copy code
from flask import Flask, jsonify, request

app = Flask(__name__)

# Mock data for demonstration
items = [{'id': i, 'name': f'Item {i}'} for i in range(1, 101)]  # 100 items

@app.route('/api/items', methods=['GET'])
def get_items():
    page = int(request.args.get('page', 1))  # Default to page 1
    per_page = int(request.args.get('per_page', 10))
  # Default to 10 items per page
    start = (page - 1) * per_page
    end = start + per_page
```

```
    paginated_items = items[start:end]
    return jsonify({
        'page': page,
        'per_page': per_page,
        'total': len(items),
        'items': paginated_items
    })

if __name__ == '__main__':
    app.run(debug=True)
```

In this example:

- The /api/items endpoint returns paginated results based on the page and per_page query parameters.
- The response includes the current page, number of items per page, total items, and the items for the requested page.

Testing Pagination

You can test pagination by accessing the endpoint with different query parameters:

```bash
Copy code
curl "http://127.0.0.1:5000/api/items?page=2&per_page=5"
```

This request will return the items for the second page with five items per page.

14.3 Implementing Webhooks with Flask

Webhooks allow your application to receive real-time updates from other services. A webhook is essentially an HTTP callback that is triggered by specific events in another application, sending data to a designated URL in your Flask app.

Step-by-Step Implementation of Webhooks

1. **Define a Webhook Endpoint**:

Create an endpoint in your Flask app to handle incoming webhook requests.
Example

```python
Copy code
@app.route('/api/webhook', methods=['POST'])
def webhook():
    data = request.json
    print(f"Received webhook data: {data}") # Log the received data
    return jsonify({'status' : 'success'}), 200
```

In this example:

- The /api/webhook endpoint listens for incoming POST requests, typically from an external service.
- The received data is logged for processing.

1. **Testing the Webhook**:

You can test the webhook using Curl or Postman by sending a POST request to the webhook endpoint with JSON data.
Example using Curl:

```bash
Copy code
curl -X POST -H "Content-Type: application/json" -d '{"event": "new_order", "order_id": 12345}' http://127.0.0.1:5000/api/webhook
```

This simulates an external service sending a webhook notification to your application.

14.4 API Throttling and Resource Limiting

Throttling and resource limiting are techniques to control the usage of API resources by clients. This is crucial for preventing abuse, ensuring fair usage, and maintaining the performance of your API.

Implementing API Throttling

You can use Flask-Limiter to manage throttling in your Flask application.
Example:

```python
Copy code
from flask_limiter import Limiter

limiter = Limiter(app, key_func=get_remote_address)

@app.route('/api/resource')
@limiter.limit("5 per minute")
# Limit to 5 requests per minute per IP
def resource():
    return jsonify({'message': 'This resource is throttled!'})
```

In this example:

- The /api/resource endpoint allows a maximum of five requests per minute per client IP.

Resource Limiting with Flask-Limiter

Resource limiting ensures that clients do not exceed their allocated resources, protecting your API from overload.
Example:

```python
Copy code
```

```
@app.route('/api/limited_resource')
@limiter.limit("10 per hour")
 # Limit to 10 requests per hour
def limited_resource():
    return jsonify({'message':
'Access granted to limited resource!'})
```

14.5 Building GraphQL APIs with Flask

GraphQL is a query language for APIs that allows clients to request specific data structures, reducing over-fetching and under-fetching issues often seen with REST APIs. Flask-GraphQL is an extension that enables you to build GraphQL APIs easily.

Step-by-Step Implementation of a GraphQL API

Step 1: Install Flask-GraphQL:

```
bash
Copy code
pip install Flask-GraphQL
```

Step 2: Define Your GraphQL Schema:

Create a simple GraphQL schema for your Flask app.

Example:

```
python
Copy code
from flask import Flask
from flask_graphql import GraphQLView
from graphene import ObjectType, String, Schema

class User(ObjectType):
    id = String()
    name = String()

class Query(ObjectType):
    user = String(id=String(required=True))
```

```
    def resolve_user(self, info, id):
        return f'User {id}'

schema = Schema(query=Query)

app = Flask(__name__)
app.add_url_rule('/graphql', view_func=GraphQLView.as_view
('graphql', schema=schema, graphiql=True)

if __name__ == '__main__':
    app.run(debug=True)
```

In this example:

- We define a simple User type and a query to resolve user data.
- The /graphql endpoint provides an interactive GraphiQL interface for testing queries.

Querying the GraphQL API

You can test the GraphQL API using the GraphiQL interface by visiting http://127.0.0.1:5000/graphql. You can run queries like:

```graphql
Copy code
{
  user(id: "1")
}
```

This query will resolve and return the corresponding user data.

Chapter 15: Version Control and CI/CD for Flask APIs

In modern software development, version control and continuous integration/continuous delivery (CI/CD) are essential practices that enhance collaboration, improve code quality, and streamline deployment processes. This chapter focuses on integrating Git for version control in Flask API projects, setting up CI with GitHub Actions, automating testing in CI/CD pipelines, and deploying updates with continuous delivery.

15.1 Integrating Git and Version Control for Flask API Projects

Git is a distributed version control system that allows developers to track changes in their codebase, collaborate effectively, and manage different versions of their projects.

Setting Up Git for Your Flask Project

1. **Initialize a Git Repository**:

- In your Flask project directory, run:

```bash
Copy code
```

CHAPTER 15: VERSION CONTROL AND CI/CD FOR FLASK APIS

```
git init
```

1. **Create a .gitignore File**:

- To exclude certain files and directories from version control (such as virtual environments and temporary files), create a .gitignore file. Example .gitignore:

```plaintext
Copy code
__pycache__/
instance/
.env
venv/
*.pyc
```

1. **Track Changes**:

- Add files to the staging area:

```bash
Copy code
git add .
```

- Commit changes with a descriptive message:

```
bash
Copy code
git commit -m "Initial commit"
```

1. **Creating Branches**:

- Use branches to develop features or fix bugs without affecting the main codebase.

```
bash
Copy code
git checkout -b feature/new-feature
```

1. **Merging Changes**:

- After completing work on a branch, merge it back into the main branch:

```
bash
Copy code
git checkout main
git merge feature/new-feature
```

15.2 Setting Up Continuous Integration with GitHub Actions

GitHub Actions is a powerful CI/CD tool that enables you to automate workflows directly from your GitHub repository. You can set up workflows to build, test, and deploy your Flask API automatically.

Step-by-Step Setup of GitHub Actions

1. **Create a Workflow File**:

- In your Flask project, create a directory for workflows:

```bash
Copy code
mkdir -p .github/workflows
```

- Create a YAML file for your workflow (e.g., ci.yml).

1. **Define the Workflow**: Example ci.yml:

```yaml
Copy code
name: CI

on:
  push:
    branches:
      - main
  pull_request:
    branches:
      - main

jobs:
  test:
    runs-on: ubuntu-latest

    steps:
      - name: Checkout code
        uses: actions/checkout@v2

      - name: Set up Python
        uses: actions/setup-python@v2
        with:
          python-version: '3.9'
```

```
     - name: Install dependencies
       run: |
         python -m pip install --upgrade pip
         pip install -r requirements.txt

     - name: Run tests
       run: |
         pytest  # Replace with your test command
```

In this example:

- The workflow triggers on pushes and pull requests to the main branch.
- It checks out the code, sets up Python, installs dependencies, and runs tests using pytest.

1. **Push Changes to GitHub**:

- Commit and push your changes to GitHub:

```
bash
Copy code
git add .github/workflows/ci.yml
git commit -m "Set up CI with GitHub Actions"
git push origin main
```

Once pushed, GitHub Actions will automatically run the defined workflow whenever you push changes or create pull requests.

15.3 Automating API Testing in CI/CD Pipelines

Automating tests in your CI/CD pipeline ensures that your Flask API remains reliable and stable as you make changes.

Step-by-Step Automation of Testing

1. **Create Test Cases**:

CHAPTER 15: VERSION CONTROL AND CI/CD FOR FLASK APIS

- Ensure you have a suite of tests for your Flask API, ideally using a testing framework like unittest or pytest.

1. **Integrate Testing in GitHub Actions**:

- Modify the workflow file (ci.yml) to include steps for running tests.

Example:

```yaml
Copy code
- name: Run tests
  run: |
    pytest tests/  # Assuming your tests are in a directory named 'tests'
```

1. **Run Tests on Every Push**:

- The modified workflow will automatically run tests every time you push code or create a pull request, ensuring that only code that passes all tests can be merged into the main branch.

1. **Fail the Build on Test Failures**:

- If any test fails, the CI/CD pipeline will fail, preventing the code from being merged until the issues are resolved.

15.4 Deploying Updates with Continuous Delivery

Continuous Delivery (CD) allows you to automatically deploy updates to your Flask API after successful tests in the CI pipeline. This ensures that your API is always in a deployable state.

Step-by-Step Implementation of Continuous Delivery

1. **Extend the GitHub Actions Workflow**:

- Add a deployment step to your existing workflow. Depending on where you are deploying (e.g., Heroku, AWS, DigitalOcean), the commands will vary.

Example for deploying to Heroku:

```yaml
Copy code
deploy:
  runs-on: ubuntu-latest
  needs: test  # Ensure tests pass before deploying
  steps:
    - name: Checkout code
      uses: actions/checkout@v2

    - name: Deploy to Heroku
      uses: akhileshns/heroku-deploy@v0.5.0
      with:
        heroku_app_name: your-app-name
        heroku_api_key: ${{ secrets.HEROKU_API_KEY }}
```

In this example:

- The needs: test ensures that the deployment job runs only after the test job completes successfully.
- The Heroku deploy step uses a GitHub action to deploy your app.

1. **Store Secrets Securely**:

- Use GitHub Secrets to store sensitive information like your Heroku API key. This can be configured in your GitHub repository settings under "Secrets".

1. **Test the Deployment**:

- Push changes to your main branch and monitor the Actions tab on GitHub to ensure that the CI/CD pipeline runs successfully and deploys your application.

Chapter 16: Monitoring and Logging Flask APIs

Monitoring and logging are essential practices for maintaining the reliability, performance, and security of APIs. They enable developers to track the application's behavior, diagnose issues, and gather insights into usage patterns. This chapter explores API monitoring, implementing logging in Flask, integrating third-party monitoring tools, setting up alerts for failures, and collecting API analytics and metrics.

16.1 Introduction to API Monitoring

API Monitoring refers to the process of tracking the performance, availability, and functionality of your API in real-time. Effective monitoring allows you to:

- **Detect Issues Early**: Identify problems before they impact users.
- **Ensure Reliability**: Monitor uptime and performance to maintain a reliable service.
- **Understand Usage Patterns**: Analyze how clients interact with your API to make informed decisions about enhancements or optimizations.

Key Metrics to Monitor

- **Response Times**: Measure how long it takes for the API to respond to

requests.
- **Error Rates**: Track the percentage of requests that result in errors.
- **Uptime**: Monitor the availability of the API over time.
- **Traffic Volume**: Analyze the number of requests received over specific time intervals.

16.2 Implementing Logging with Flask-Logging

Flask-Logging is an extension that provides easy logging capabilities for Flask applications. Proper logging is essential for diagnosing issues and understanding application behavior.

Step-by-Step Implementation of Logging

Step 1: Install Flask-Logging (if not using the built-in logging):

```
bash
Copy code
pip install Flask-Logging
```

Step 2: Configure Logging in Your Flask App:

```
python
Copy code
import logging
from flask import Flask

app = Flask(__name__)

# Configure logging
logging.basicConfig(level=logging.INFO,
format='%(asctime)s -
 %(name)s - %(levelname)s - %(message)s')

@app.route('/api/resource', methods=['GET'])
def get_resource():
    app.logger.
info('Resource accessed')
```

```
    return {'data':
'This is your resource'}

if __name__ == '__main__':
    app.run(debug=True)
```

In this example:

- The logging level is set to INFO, so all messages at this level and above will be logged.
- The format specifies how log messages should appear, including timestamps, the logger's name, the severity level, and the actual message.

Step 3: Logging Errors and Exceptions:
You can also log errors and exceptions that occur in your application:

```python
Copy code
@app.erro-handler(500)
def internal_server_error(error):
    app.logger.error(f'Server Error: {error}')
    return {'error':
'Internal Server Error'}, 500
```

This logs the error message whenever a 500 Internal Server Error occurs, providing valuable information for debugging.

16.3 Integrating Third-Party Monitoring Tools

To gain deeper insights into your API's performance and behavior, consider integrating third-party monitoring tools. These tools can provide advanced analytics, alerting, and visualization capabilities.

Popular Monitoring Tools

1. **New Relic**: Offers performance monitoring, error tracking, and detailed transaction traces.

2. **Datadog**: Provides real-time monitoring, dashboards, and alerting capabilities.
3. **Prometheus and Grafana**: Open-source monitoring and alerting toolkit with powerful visualization capabilities.

Example: Integrating New Relic

1. **Install the New Relic Python Agent**:

```bash
Copy code
pip install newrelic
```

1. **Create a New Relic Configuration File**:

```bash
Copy code
newrelic-admin generate-config
YOUR_NEW_RELIC_LICENSE_KEY
 newrelic.ini
```

1. **Run Your Flask Application with New Relic**:

```bash
Copy code
NEW_RELIC_CONFIG_FILE=newrelic.
ini newrelic-admin run-program python app.py
```

In this example:

- The New Relic agent tracks application performance and sends data to your New Relic dashboard.

16.4 Setting Up Alerts for API Failures

Setting up alerts is crucial for proactive monitoring of your API. Alerts notify developers of issues in real time, allowing for quick responses to potential problems.

Steps to Set Up Alerts

1. **Define Alert Criteria**:

- Determine what conditions should trigger alerts, such as:
- High error rates (e.g., more than 5% of requests fail)
- Increased response times (e.g., average response time exceeds 2 seconds)
- Server downtime or unavailability

1. **Configure Alerts in Monitoring Tools**:

- Most third-party monitoring tools have built-in alerting features. For example, in New Relic, you can set up alert policies based on your defined criteria.

1. **Integrate Notification Channels**:

- Configure notification channels (e.g., email, Slack, SMS) to receive alerts. Ensure that the right team members are notified when issues arise.

16.5 API Analytics and Metrics

Collecting and analyzing API metrics is vital for understanding usage patterns and making data-driven decisions for enhancements and optimizations.

Key Metrics to Collect

1. **Traffic Metrics**:

CHAPTER 16: MONITORING AND LOGGING FLASK APIS

- Total number of requests per endpoint
- Requests per user or IP address

1. **Performance Metrics**:

- Average response time
- Error rates and response codes

1. **Usage Patterns**:

- Peak usage times (to plan for scaling)
- Most frequently accessed endpoints

Implementing Metrics Collection

You can manually log metrics in your application or use third-party tools for automated collection and visualization.

Example: Logging Traffic Metrics

```python
Copy code
@app.route('/api/resource', methods=['GET'])
def get_resource():
    app.logger.info('Resource accessed', extra={'request_count': 1})
    return {'data': 'This is your resource'}
```

You can then aggregate and analyze these logs with tools like ELK Stack (Elasticsearch, Logstash, Kibana) or integrate with analytics services like Google Analytics.

Chapter 17: Scaling Flask APIs

As your Flask API grows in usage and complexity, it becomes essential to scale the application to handle increased traffic and ensure reliability. This chapter explores various strategies for scaling Flask APIs, including the use of load balancers, microservices architecture, caching and queueing systems, managing traffic spikes, and optimizing performance for high demand.

17.1 Scaling Flask APIs with Load Balancers

Load Balancers are critical components in distributed systems that distribute incoming network traffic across multiple servers to ensure no single server becomes overwhelmed. This approach improves availability and reliability while optimizing resource use.

Key Benefits of Load Balancing

- **Improved Reliability**: If one server fails, the load balancer can redirect traffic to healthy servers.
- **Increased Throughput**: Distributing requests across multiple servers can enhance the overall throughput of the application.
- **Scalability**: Adding more servers to handle increased load becomes straightforward.

Implementing Load Balancing for Flask APIs

CHAPTER 17: SCALING FLASK APIS

1. **Deploy Multiple Instances of Your Flask Application**:

- Use a process manager like Gunicorn to run multiple instances of your Flask app.

```bash
Copy code
gunicorn -w 4 -b 0.0.0.0:5000 app:app  # Run 4 worker processes
```

1. **Set Up a Load Balancer**:

- You can use a software load balancer like **NGINX** or a cloud-based load balancer provided by services like AWS Elastic Load Balancing (ELB).
- Example NGINX configuration for load balancing:

```nginx
Copy code
upstream flask_app {
    server app_server1:5000;
    server app_server2:5000;
    server app_server3:5000;
}

server {
    listen 80;

    location / {
        proxy_pass http://flask_app;
        proxy_set_header Host $host;
        proxy_set_header X-Real-IP $remote_addr;
        proxy_set_header X-Forwarded-For $proxy_add_x_forwarded_for;
```

```
        proxy_set_header
X-Forwarded-Proto $scheme;
    }
}
```

In this configuration:

- Incoming requests to the load balancer are distributed among multiple Flask app instances.

17.2 Horizontal Scaling with Microservices Architecture

Horizontal Scaling involves adding more instances of a service rather than upgrading the existing hardware (vertical scaling). One effective way to achieve horizontal scaling is through **Microservices Architecture**, where the application is broken down into smaller, independently deployable services.

Key Benefits of Microservices

- **Decoupled Services**: Each service can be developed, deployed, and scaled independently.
- **Technology Agnostic**: Different services can use different technologies, allowing for flexibility in choosing the right tools for each task.
- **Easier Scaling**: Services can be scaled based on their individual demand rather than scaling the entire application.

Implementing Microservices Architecture

1. **Identify Services**: Break down your application into smaller services based on business functionality (e.g., user management, order processing, payment).
2. **API Communication**: Use REST or GraphQL for communication between services. Consider message brokers like RabbitMQ or Kafka for asynchronous communication.

3. **Deploy Each Service Independently**: Use containers (e.g., Docker) to deploy each service in isolation, ensuring consistency across environments.

17.3 Implementing Caching and Queueing Systems

Caching and **Queueing** are powerful strategies to optimize API performance and manage workloads effectively.

Caching

Caching stores copies of files or data temporarily to speed up future requests. This reduces the load on your servers and improves response times.

1. **Use Flask-Caching**: Implement caching in your Flask app to cache responses or expensive computations.
2. **Backend Caching Systems**: Use Redis or Memcached as caching backends for more complex caching needs.

Example:

```python
Copy code
from flask_caching import Cache

cache = Cache(app, config={'CACHE_TYPE': 'redis'})

@app.route('/api/data')
@cache.cached(timeout=60)
def get_data():
    return {'data': 'This is cached data'}
```

Queueing

Queueing allows you to handle long-running tasks asynchronously without blocking the API responses.

1. **Use a Queueing System**: Implement tools like **Celery** with a message broker (RabbitMQ or Redis) to manage background tasks.

Example:

```python
Copy code
from celery import Celery

app = Flask(__name__)
celery = Celery(app.name, broker='redis://localhost:6379/0')

@celery.task
def long_running_task(data):
    # Perform a long-running task
    return "Task complete!"

@app.route('/api/async-task', methods=['POST'])
def run_task():
    data = request.json
    task = long_running_task.apply_async(args=[data])
    return jsonify({'task_id': task.id}), 202
```

17.4 Managing Traffic Spikes and High Demand

When an API experiences sudden increases in traffic, it can lead to performance degradation or outages. Managing traffic spikes effectively is crucial for maintaining service reliability.

Strategies for Handling Traffic Spikes

1. **Auto-Scaling**: Utilize cloud provider features (e.g., AWS Auto Scaling, Google Cloud Autoscaler) to automatically adjust the number of running instances based on demand.
2. **Load Testing**: Use tools like **Apache JMeter** or **Gatling** to simulate high traffic and assess your API's performance under load.
3. **Implement Rate Limiting**: Use Flask-Limiter to control the number of requests from individual users during peak times.
4. **Use a Content Delivery Network (CDN)**: For serving static assets, a CDN can help distribute the load and reduce latency for users across different geographic locations.

17.5 Optimizing Flask for High Performance

To ensure your Flask API performs well under load, consider the following optimization strategies:

1. **Profile Your Application**:

- Use profiling tools (e.g., Flask-DebugToolbar) to identify performance bottlenecks in your application.

1. **Use a Production WSGI Server**:

- Deploy your Flask app using a production-ready WSGI server like Gunicorn or uWSGI instead of the built-in Flask server.

1. **Database Optimization**:

- Optimize database queries by using indexes and minimizing the number of queries. Consider using a connection pool to manage database connections efficiently.

1. **Optimize Middleware**:

- Minimize the use of middleware that adds latency to your requests. Use only necessary middleware to keep response times low.

1. **Minimize Response Size**:

- Reduce the size of the API responses by limiting the amount of data sent to clients and using efficient data formats (e.g., JSON over XML).

1. **Use Compression**:

- Enable response compression (e.g., gzip) to reduce the size of the data sent over the network.

Example of enabling gzip compression in Flask:

```python
Copy code
from flask import Flask
from flask_compress import Compress

app = Flask(__name__)
Compress(app)
```

By the end of this chapter, you should have a solid understanding of various strategies for scaling Flask APIs. We explored how to use load balancers, implement microservices architecture, utilize caching and queueing systems, manage traffic spikes, and optimize Flask for high performance. These practices will enable your API to handle increased demand while maintaining reliability and responsiveness.

Chapter 18: Conclusion and Next Steps

In this concluding chapter, we will summarize the key concepts covered throughout the book, outline actionable next steps for API developers, discuss ways to expand your API with additional features, and recommend valuable resources for continued learning in Flask API development.

18.1 Summary of Key Concepts

Throughout this book, we have explored various aspects of building and managing Flask APIs, including:

1. **API Development Fundamentals**: Understanding what APIs are, different types, and how to create a basic API using Flask.
2. **Setting Up Flask**: Installation and basic app structure, including creating API endpoints and handling requests.
3. **Database Integration**: Connecting Flask applications to databases using SQLAlchemy, performing CRUD operations, and handling migrations.
4. **Error Handling and Security**: Implementing error handling, authentication, and authorization for secure API access.
5. **Advanced Features**: Using Flask-SocketIO for real-time communication, implementing pagination, handling file uploads and downloads, and building GraphQL APIs.
6. **Monitoring and Logging**: Establishing effective logging and monitor-

ing strategies to track API performance and diagnose issues.
7. **Scaling and Performance**: Strategies for scaling Flask APIs, including load balancing, caching, and optimizing performance for high traffic.
8. **Version Control and CI/CD**: Integrating Git for version control, setting up continuous integration with GitHub Actions, and automating deployment processes.

18.2 Next Steps for API Developers

As you move forward with your journey in API development, consider the following next steps:

1. **Build a Real-World Project**: Apply what you've learned by developing a complete API project. This could be anything from a simple RESTful API to a more complex application using microservices architecture.
2. **Contribute to Open Source**: Join open-source projects that interest you. This will help you gain experience, learn from others, and contribute to the community.
3. **Stay Updated**: Keep an eye on new developments in Flask and the broader web development ecosystem. New tools, best practices, and frameworks continue to evolve.

18.3 Expanding Your API with Additional Features

Once you have a foundational API, consider implementing additional features to enhance its functionality:

1. **API Versioning**: Implement versioning to manage changes to your API without breaking existing client implementations.
2. **Rate Limiting and Throttling**: Enhance your API's security and performance by controlling how clients can access your resources.
3. **Documentation**: Utilize tools like Swagger or OpenAPI to create comprehensive documentation that helps clients understand how to use your API effectively.
4. **Enhanced Security Measures**: Explore advanced authentication

methods (e.g., OAuth2, JWT) and implement secure data handling practices to protect user data.

18.4 Recommended Resources for Flask API Development

To further your knowledge and skills in Flask API development, consider the following resources:

1. **Books**:

- *Flask Web Development* by Miguel Grinberg: A comprehensive guide to building web applications using Flask.
- *Flask by Example* by Gareth Dwyer: A hands-on approach to building practical applications with Flask.

1. **Online Courses**:

- **Udemy**: Various courses on Flask development, covering everything from basics to advanced topics.
- **Coursera**: Courses that focus on web development and APIs using Python and Flask.

1. **Documentation**:

- Flask Documentation: The official documentation is an excellent resource for learning about Flask and its extensions.
- Flask-RESTful Documentation: For learning about building RESTful APIs with Flask-RESTful.

1. **Community and Forums**:

- **Stack Overflow**: A valuable resource for asking questions and finding answers related to Flask and API development.
- **Flask Discord Community**: Join the Flask community on Discord to

interact with other developers, share knowledge, and seek help.

www.ingramcontent.com/pod-product-compliance
Lightning Source LLC
Chambersburg PA
CBHW050000230526
45465CB00003BB/1182